# The
# Hampshire
# Village Book

# The Hampshire Village Book

## ANTHONY BRODE

with illustrations by R. C. Garman

COUNTRYSIDE BOOKS

NEWBURY

First Published 1980

Revised Edition 1983

© Anthony Brode 1980
All rights reserved. No reproduction
permitted without the
prior permission of the publishers:
Countryside Books
3 Catherine Road, Newbury, Berkshire

ISBN 0 905392 06 X

Designed by Mon Mohan

Map of Hampshire drawn by David Thelwell

The cover photograph of Buriton pond is reproduced
by kind permission of Hampshire County Council
Planning Department.

Printed in Great Britain by
J.W. Arrowsmith Ltd, Bristol

For Alison and Nicholas—
with another drop of Chaucer:
"Know thy contree!"
(The Balade de Bon Conseyl)

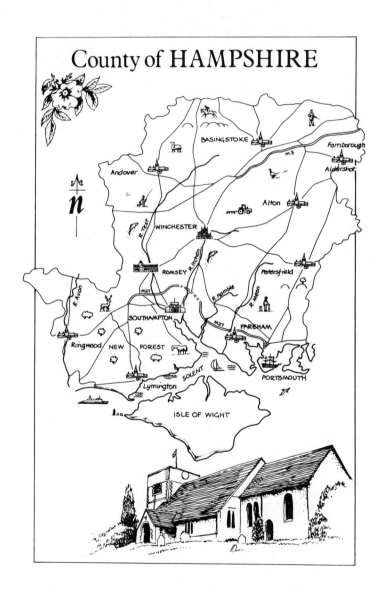

# County of HAMPSHIRE

BASINGSTOKE
Farnborough
M3
Aldershot
Andover
Alton
N
R. Test
WINCHESTER
ROMSEY
R. Itchen
Petersfield
R. Avon
M27
R. Hamble
R. Meon
SOUTHAMPTON
M27
FAREHAM
Ringwood
NEW
FOREST
PORTSMOUTH
SOLENT
Lymington
ISLE OF WIGHT

# Foreword

This book is a felicitous marriage of writer and subject. Tony Brode visited many of the villages of Hampshire in the way of his journalistic business. He was not simply a tourist, nor a self-indulgent romantic; he went to observe and, often unknowingly, to study. Meanwhile, as background, his natural literary bent led him to read the subject pleasurably in his spare time. He has a feeling for atmosphere, an eye for detail and an ear for the relevant anecdote.

He was wise in his choice; for the villages are far nearer the heart of Hampshire than the towns; most of which are in the county, but not of it. Thus Portsmouth is Royal Navy, looking out to the path of the warships and forward to retirement, and leaving Britain's only, and now often lonely, island city. Southampton, which gazed out along the paths of the ocean passenger liners, still has its eye seaward for the cruise ships, the channel ferries, Channel Island boats and the container craft. Aldershot and Farnborough are military posting towns; Basingstoke and Andover, London overspill areas. These have few roots in Hampshire.

The villages, though—especially those of the New Forest and the central highlands, which have not been swamped by the outsprawl of Portsmouth and Southampton— retain much of their old charm; indeed, in many cases are more visually pleasing than in their more natural phase.

Mr Brode is all but too late to catch the true village life of the county. It is within living memory that villages were busy places; the smoke of the fire, the wheeze of the bellows, thud of hammer and smell of burning hooves came from the smithy. Outside the village store one or another of the horse carts was being loaded for its delivery round to the remote farms. The lanes were rarely empty: for those who lived in the village worked and had their being there. On Mondays cottage gardens were whitely plentiful with washing; with housewives bustling out to the clothes line and back to a kitchen, from which came the smell of cooking—especially boiling bacon or baking cakes. The back garden held its pig, if all was well, with a litter; a cluck-chattering chicken run and enough cabbage and potatoes to last best part of the year round, and a couple of elderly apple trees. The thatched roof was dowdy but still—just—waterproof; the lime wash dull, the door sagged on its hinges and the lead-lights of the windows were slightly buckled. The men who lived in them were farm labourers or sometimes smallholders; gardeners from the big house, or small tradesmen.

Now all that has changed. Modern farming methods, large fields, few hedges, mechanical milking, silos, tractors for all work, have reduced the numbers of workers. The late 'thirties but, above all, the 'forties and 'fifties, saw a steady drain away from the villages to the higher wages and indoor employment of the towns. The workers who remain have opted for new semi-detacheds with bathrooms and garages. As a result the cottages have passed to retired people; weekenders; increasingly, latterly, to urban workers in search of a rustic dormitory, all of whom maintain them in such a whitewashed and freshly thatched—sometimes carriage-lamped and plaster-dwarfed—state of smartness as their original occupants barely thought of, and certainly could not afford.

Still the typical South-country core of church, manor house, manor farm, vicarage, and often pond, village green, schoolhouse, and a petrol pump where the smithy used to be, remain the hub of the village.

Still, too, much of rustic charm, backwater calm and ancient tradition can be observed, recorded and preserved; Tony Brode has done that with sincerity and enthusiasm.

John Arlott
Alresford
May 1980

# Author's Note

This is not primarily a guidebook. It will not tell you where to leave the motorway for the hamlets of Loose Chippings and Chipping St Osmond, or which days Balsam Friary is open to the public, or where to find the crustiest apple crumble between Hammersmith and Honiton.

The ensuing pages concentrate on the feel rather than the appearance of a village. In place of geography and gastronomy, uplift and architecture there is a little history, a pinch of legend, the odd anecdote, and a good deal of individual reminiscence.

I began to get to know Hampshire—the process is still continuing—in 1941 as the youngest and greenest member of the editorial staff of the *Farnham, Haslemere & Hindhead Herald, Alton Mail, Bordon & Longmoor Journal, Liphook & Liss News* and *North Sussex Advertiser* (it was all one paper). This involved bicycling round various villages asking what had happened since my visit of the previous week. Often, nothing had.

When I passed on this non-information to the chief reporter, Mr Percy Day, or the editor-proprietor, Mr Ernest Langham, I was seldom believed. This is understandable since the *Herald*—now a much more impressive publication—then thrived largely on very small paragraphs in very small type about very small events gathered by Stella Eldridge, Daphne Oxenford and myself from parsonages and post-offices, courts and cottages, manors and farmhouses, and the premises of undertakers and agricultural contractors. Percy did the big stuff, such as urban council meetings.

Stints on other newspapers and in television and radio, still based in Hampshire, followed. Absence only made the heart grow fonder. Working for a while in London, I could see from the BBC's External Services newsroom in Bush House a short stretch of the Thames, and drew comfort from the thought that a minute proportion of it had started off at Selborne. But an Editor for the Day told me I spent too much time looking out of the window; and then a new office building, as though at his command—pretty powerful characters, these Editors for the

Day—rose up and blocked out the river. It was time to return to Hampshire.

Among my predecessors in writing about the county was John Norden. He offered the results of his research to the public in 1625 with the plea

*Beare with Defectes*!

I couldn't have put it better myself.

Frogham: May 1980

Postscript, February 1983. Reprinting provides an opportunity to make good a number of "defectes": the Morant Hall at Brockenhurst, for instance, was very sneakily (from my point of view) demolished while I was working in London. Still, as the "New Milton Advertiser" sternly pointed out, Mr. Brode is a journalist and should check his facts . . . his grammar, too: purists will be relieved that the component parts of an infinitive inadvertently split on page 23 of the original are now happily reunited.

A generous review in the county magazine "Hampshire" accurately observed that a lot more material was available than I had used, and the writer suggested a better title might have been something along the lines of "Brode's Hampshire Villages". However, when I read – and enjoyed – "James Herriott's Yorkshire" I remember thinking "Dammit, it's my Yorkshire too!" This book is in any case something of a co-operative effort and I have now been able to include additional information which readers were kind enough to send me when it first came out.

A.B.

# Abbotts Ann ❧

When Miss Lily Myra Annetts died at Abbotts Ann in 1973 the mourners maintained a tradition by carrying a virgin's crown in the funeral procession. It had been made on a hazel frame by a long-serving churchwarden, Jesse Threadgill, who luckily had some twigs left over from one he had made 20 years previously for Miss Elizabeth Jane Wisewell. Older parishioners recalled that when Miss Annetts' brother William George died at the age of 15 in 1918 he, too, had been accompanied to the church by the Crown reserved for parishioners with unblemished reputations. During the compilation of this book it was decided to erect a plaque in the church in memory of Mr Threadgill, who died in 1978 after 50 years as a parish councillor and 32 on Andover Rural Council—of which he was chairman for a record 21 years.

Known locally as garlands, the white mitre-like paper crowns or chaplets are decorated not only with rosettes but—in case anyone should wish to challenge the reputation of the dear departed—by cut-out gauntlets. Only those born in the parish qualify: Miss Wisewell achieved the right to be considered by some 72 hours, having arrived in the world only three days after her mother had arrived in Abbotts Ann. The custom was for the "garland" to be carried in front of the coffin hanging from a rod held by two girls dressed in white. It was suspended near the west end of the church so that everybody passed underneath it, and then placed on an inside wall of the church with a shield giving the appropriate name, age and date. The earliest is believed to have been put up in the middle of the 18th century, not long after the building of the church.

Among the first inhabitants of the area were the Atrebates, a Belgic tribe said to have literally broken new ground with the introduction of an eight-oxpower plough. The next big breakthrough came when William Tasker invented a revolutionary swivel-headed plough some 19 centuries later.

The village school was established in 1831 by a rector, the Reverend Samuel Best, on a site leased from the Lord of the Manor, his brother Thomas. A plaque recording the headteachers' names (the first was its founder) was unveiled by a descendant, Tom de Paravicini, in 1978.

Another link with the past had been established in the previous year when Peter Young, a Cornish businessman, contributed generously to the repair of a stained glass window in the church. He was a descendant of Walter Young, who lived in a thatched cottage he built himself and was for many years the village shoemaker and cobbler. His parents John and Jane had been awarded 4s from parish funds in 1838 so that they could buy enough leather to make him a pair of shoes.

When times were better in the early years of this century Abbots Ann boasted a skin-and-wind band, formed by Alfred Whimpey, whose members subscribed twopence a week and met for practice in Jarvey Potter's coach-house. Alfred's son Leonard recalled in retirement at Winchester in 1965 not only the musicians' first performance in public—it was at a wedding reception and by the time it finished only four bandsmen were sober enough to play—but its last. This was an alfresco concert on Boxing Day 1905, which concluded in a somewhat disorderly display of countermarching in a cornfield. However, one of the three drummers was Roland Parfitt, later a much-respected member of the Andover Temperance Band.

There is no suggestion that alcohol played any significant part in various sightings of a ghostly coach-and-four on the road to Red Rice, and of a large black dog at various points in the village.

# Alresford ✤

Town or village? Old Alresford is certainly the latter, and Broad Street gives New Alresford a villagey appearance. When I was a young reporter it was the parish (not town) council I attended—come on, let's cheat a little. And incidentally the derivation is "the ford by the alders" (dialect forms of alder are aller and oller). Whoever thought of calling one of the Itchen feeder streams the Alre produced a pronunciation problem not entirely solved by the later version "Arle".

A photograph still exists of a group of ladies, in stern late-Victorian black from high bonnets to buttoned boots, who were the first members of the Mothers' Union. The organisation was founded by the wife of a rector of Old Alresford, the Reverend George Sumner. The Sumners had a lot of ground to make up: the previous incumbent, His Reverence the Earl of Guildford, had diverted enough funds from a Winchester charity he controlled to enlarge his already handsome rectory. It overlooks an earlier piece of ecclesiastical enterprise, a reservoir created by a 12th-century Bishop of Winchester, de Lucy, as headwater for a navigation to connect Alresford, Winchester, and Southampton. Four hundred years later Leland described it as "a good brode lak communely called Alsford Pond". Now somewhat shrunken, it is devoted to wildfowl and watercress. The road across the causeway which holds back the water connects Old Alresford with New—though the latter was replanned by that same de Lucy eight centuries ago—where the connections are literary rather than ecclesiastical.

The novelist Mary Russell Mitford was born in 1787 in one of the elegant houses which still line Broad Street. She thought Jane Austen (see Chawton) "the prettiest, silliest, husband-hunting butterfly" whose work was "deficient in both taste and a perception of the graceful". In the churchyard is buried John Freemantle, poet, astronomer, shoe-maker, newspaper reporter, sign-writer and will-maker. It is recorded that his charge for drawing up a will was one shilling, and that "in no case was one disputed". In his old age, Queen Victoria sent him fifty guineas.

Freemantle was also the name of one of four Alresford men—the others were Taylor, Benham, and Dunn—who played for Hambledon Cricket Club in its heyday. This prompted another pronouncement from Mary Russell Mitford, who claimed: "Cricket is to Alresford what beer is to Doncaster or cakes to Shrewsbury: Hampshire is the Greece of cricket and Alresford the Athens."

In medieval times it was also a bit of a Bradford in its way, prospering through the wool trade. There are said to have been four fulling mills—as well as six corn mills—within a mile, and Alresford Sheep Fair survived into the present century.

Despite ready supplies of water the history of New Alresford has been punctuated by fires. Of four in the 17th century the least disastrous was deliberately started by Royalist troops after their defeat on the high ground south of Alresford (see Cheriton).

Another battle was fought over the closure of the Mid-Hants line, which joined Alton and Winchester and was used by London–Southampton trains in times of war, breakdown and other emergency. Eloquent campaigners to keep Alresford's rail link included Mr John Taylor, then deputy clerk to Winchester Rural Council, and Mr John Arlott, whose home for many years was a former pub, the Old Sun, at the Alton end of the main street. The line, opened in 1865, was closed in 1973 despite the fact that it was losing only £2,000 a year before staff and freight-service cuts saved £6,000 a year; was used daily by 170 schoolchildren; and took commuters to Winchester, Eastleigh, and Southampton.

Among British Rail's tactics listed by Mr Arlott at the time were: Making watercress growers (who provided much of the line's freight and gave it its nickname) pay their bills in such a way that the money would not be credited to the line's finances; requiring them to load their produce on to a railway lorry which took it by road to Basingstoke; using three-car trains which had no corridors, so that the conductors introduced as an economy measure could not collect all the fares; turning back to Waterloo any Alton-bound train that was 10 minutes late at Farnham; and cutting out all those Waterloo–Alton Sunday trains which connected at Alton with the Mid-Hants! Plans for a scheduled service to be run by private enterprise fell though but Alresford Station still sees crowded platforms when preservationists run steam-hauled trains along a truncated stretch of the line.

In the mid-1940s there was, I admit, a 100-year-old building known firmly as the Town Hall. It survived as a community centre. When I frequented it, there was a small room used for political and other meetings. Women members of the East Hants Conservative Association whose proceedings I reported used to applaud speakers not by clapping but by scraping the floor with their feet.

14

The main hall was used on some evenings for dancing and on some mornings as a magistrates' court. This is why the members of the Bench—I don't know what effect their appearance had on the defendants, but in the Press seats I often feared instant transportation—sat beneath a notice saying NO JITTERBUGGING.

# Amport ✑

> Late supping I forbear;
> Wine and women I forswear;
> My neck and feet I keep from cold;
> No marvel then though I be old.
> I am a willow, not an oak;
> I chide but never hurt with stroke.

The man who wrote these lines in his journal died in 1577 at the age of 97, "having seen 103 persons descended from him". He was Sir William Paulet, Lord of the Manor of Amport, created first Marquis of Winchester in 1551. The first recorded landowner was Hugh de Port (the village gets its name partly from him, partly from the River Ann), whose Domesday Book holdings included vast tracts of what is now Hampshire. The manor house, rebuilt after the Elizabethan mansion had been destroyed by fire, was the Headquarters of RAF Maintenance Command from 1939 until 1960, when it became a training centre for RAF chaplains.

Perhaps their presence might have had a salutary effect some hundred years previously, when the parish operated what were a kind of almshouses-in-reverse. For in "Quality Square" (who says sick jokes are an invention of the present century?) were maintained dwellings "into which were installed persons whom the churchwardens thought might contaminate the more virtuous inhabitants of the village."

Finally an extract from the parish records: "November 11, 1830, will always be memorable in the annals of Amport. The labouring men rose in revolt and destroyed the machinery and demanded that their wages should be increased. As there was

15

no force to repel their violence, the employers were compelled to yield to their demands."

# Avington 🦋

"One of the very prettiest spots in the world", wrote William Cobbett in spite, or perhaps because, of the deforestation of Hampage Wood to provide timber for the building of Winchester Cathedral. One story says that its builder Walkelyn was told he could have as much timber as could be taken in one night, another in three days. Both versions agree that he assembled an army of men for the task, though there is doubt whether they removed all that was worth taking or left just a single tree. This tree used to be identified as the Gospel Oak, where an open-air service was held during Rogationtide processions (there is even the unlikely legend that St Augustine preached under its branches; by the beginning of this century only the stump was left).

In recent centuries the history of this Itchen Valley village has almost been that of the "Big House"; known variously as Old Hall or Old Avington House. Charles II stayed there, and there was a bathing-pool "made for Nell Gwynne". Pepys records that when it belonged to George Brydges his wife, Lady Shrewsbury, waited dressed as a page while he fought a duel over her with her lover, the Duke of Buckingham.

The village was much affected by the agricultural riots of 150 years ago (see Selborne) and in 1830 the Duke of Wellington was informed by the owner of Avington House—incidentally, a later Duke of Buckingham—that "this part of the country is wholly in the hands of the rebels. The rioters are to assemble tomorrow morning, and will attack any farmhouses where there are threshing machines." Perhaps what actually happened was an early attempt at secondary picketing. A mob is said to have arrived from Winchester, whereupon a local magistrate assembled a group of villagers who helped him ensure that no damage was done.

Avington Park became the property of the Shelley family, later the Shelley-Rolls. An unusual feature of the parish church is a barrel-organ provided in 1849 by Lady Shelley. Each of its two barrels has 15 tunes, hymns, and chants.

# Barton Stacey 🦚

Once a large and flourishing village with two malthouses and a brewery, it was dealt a severe blow in 1792 by what a contemporary account called "a most awful conflagration. . . . Some people being at work in Mr Moody's shop, smith and edge-tool maker, a large flake of red-hot iron flew out of the shop window, and falling on some dry litter near a cucumber-bed set it instantly on fire. This communicated to an adjoining mill-house, covered with thatch, where a horse was at work, and the whole, in a few minutes, was in flames. . . . The wind high, and blowing in a direct line with the street, carried the thatch like a storm of fire, swifter than a man could run, from one house to another, until the whole village was in flames. At one instant 27 houses, 13 barns, 10 stables, several granaries and four ricks of capital wheat were on fire. . . . Only one life was lost, and that through obstinacy. Farmer Friend, at the advanced age of 60, perished in going upstairs after money."

Barton in this instance probably means a fortified manor. This one had belonged to Edward the Confessor and remained a royal manor until 1199, when it was acquired by Rogo de Saci. In November 1978 Sotheby's sold the Letters Patent of October 1st, 1294, bearing the Great Seal of England, under which it was transferred to John Berwick, a member of the king's household, together with "all woods, meadows, pastures, rivers, fisheries, ponds, mills, paths, moors and heaths" Even today the Crown has a connection with the village in the army camp which bears its name.

# Basing (see Old Basing) 🦚

# Beaulieu 🦢

When King John made a grant of land around a wooded inlet on the Hampshire coast to the Cistercians in 1204 it was referred to as "a fine place belonging to the king", or Bellus locus regis. Bellus locus became in the monks' own language Beau lieu: but the present Lord Montagu of Beaulieu pointed out in 1970 that it was probably pronounced Bewlee (or Bewly) from the beginning, and that it was spelled Beuli on a map of 1250. He had also been told that the Norman pronunciation of Beau was still beu. His informant, a Frenchman, was glad that the English used the "proper" pronunciation!

The monks built their abbey of stone at a time when most local buildings were cob—clay mixed with heather or straw. One of the last buildings to be built of cob in the New Forest was put up near Hatchet Pond above Beaulieu village in about 1930. Roofed in corrugated metal and with "severe structural damage" it was sold in 1978 for £14,000. By contrast a five-bedroomed house built by an architect for over £200,000 not long after the war (it was faced in Spanish and Italian marble and had a split-level semicircular drawing-room overlooking Beaulieu River) was sold in 1970 for less than half it cost.

The ruinous state of Beaulieu Abbey is due less to the ravages of time than to its fate after the Dissolution. Stone was taken for the construction of Hurst Castle, and the manor was sold to Henry VIII's treasurer, the first Earl of Southampton, Thomas Wriothesley (see Titchfield), in 1528. Its great gateway was incorporated into Palace House in 1573; the refectory became the parish church, which is why the building has a north–south alignment instead of the traditional east–west.

The centuries during which the Abbey flourished have, however, left their mark on the area. A local field-name, Terre Belle, became the Derables. The Bergerie farm remains, though sometimes called Bargery. A series of monastic records, the Beaulieu Cartulary, includes in its details of rents, properties, and land dealings an account of disturbances when the monks tried to enclose waste land in the southern part of the New Forest: objectors retaliated by burning fences, uprooting hedges and filling ditches. The historian who edited the Cartulary for the Southampton Records Series says its compilation "throws little credit on the monks of Beaulieu as efficient keepers of archives".

Nevertheless much information is available from other sources. In the middle ages the abbey provided sanctuary for many debtors and felons and others pursued by the law—including Perkin Warbeck, pretender to the throne.

Parish records include details of various payments to officials. In 1674, for instance, the man who kept the roads in good order—the waywarden—was paid sixteen shillings "for laying a bunny in Tanhouse Lane". It may be necessary to add in this Playboy era that a bunny is a Hampshire dialect word for a culvert or ravine, and survives in several placenames, such as Beckton Bunny and Chewton Bunny (see Milton).

In 1726 the parish clerk was apparently allowed to charge travelling expenses. There is an entry which says: "Going to Brocknas to the spinning master, 2s." Brocknas is evidently a phonetic version of Brockenhurst.

Though the village had—at that time, at least—no spinning master of its own there are still recollections of twine and sacking being made in the last century.

Some time before 1900 a brass band was formed. It used to meet for practice at the village hall or in the mill. The bandmaster was Tom Gregory, who had been taught by his father—a member of the church band before the organ was installed. Tom and his pupil, Frank Drake, continued to play cornet for church services from time to time. It has been proudly placed on record that when various bands took part in the annual Hospital Sunday parade at Lymington, the only band that played while marching up the hill was Beaulieu's.

In 1941 the Special Operations Executive took over ten houses on the Beaulieu Manor Estate as a "finishing school" for agents after their preliminary training. A plaque in the Cloisters asks visitors to: "Remember before God these men and women of the European Resistance Movement who were secretly trained at Beaulieu to fight their lonely battle against Hitler's Germany and who, before entering Nazi-occupied territory, here found some measure of the peace for which they fought."

One monastic tradition which has been revived in an area now largely devoted to commemorating the internal combustion engine is the growing of vines. The motor museum had a head start, founded in 1952 by the present Lord Montagu with his father's 1903 de Dion Bouton as a nucleus. In 1958 2,000 German vines were planted as the result of an inspiration of Mrs Margaret Gore-Browne, wife of the late Colonel Robert Gore-Browne, then a freeholder at "Vineyards" on the Beaulieu Estate. The operation, which over the years has grown considerably, is now run by the estate itself. The archivist at Beaulieu, Mr A. J. Holland, has made the point that in Cistercian days the monks did not produce their own wine but imported it.

In 1979 Beaulieu won the under-500-population class in Hampshire's "Best-Kept-Village" competition: partly because, in the opinion of the judges, it was "not spoilt by shoddy gift shops or glaring advertisements".

Beauworth

# Beauworth

A spelling of 1284 is Beworth, and that's roughly how it is pronounced. It means bee-farm, which is perhaps why someone suggested that Beaulieu should be bee-ley or bee-meadow.

Near the crossroads on Millbarrow Down above the village is a former medieval farmhouse which for the last 200 years of its existence has been an inn, the Fox & Hounds; 634 feet above sea level, it has a 300-foot well which may date back to the 12th century. The water was raised in an 18-gallon wooden bucket. At one time a donkey provided the motive power but usually it was operated by a man walking inside a 12-foot diameter treadwheel for 12 minutes, though a record-breaker once did it in six. The gudgeons of the wheel were twice reset by landlord Freddie Hoar, who was also the village's joiner, undertaker, decorator, builder, and wheelwright. He was succeeded by his son-in-law, Jack New; and the well has been succeeded as a source of supply by water from the mains.

# Bentley 🍃

A timber "book" six feet high tells visitors something of Bentley's history, though the suggestion that it means "the green by the forest" is not always supported by today's sources of reference which prefer "a clearing overgrown by bent-grass".

The impressive history-book was commissioned by the founder of the Boy Scout movement, Lord Baden-Powell, who lived near by at Pax Hill for 19 years before leaving England for Kenya. Its "brief chronicles" include the coming of the Romans in AD 41, and in fact the first evidence of local industry is provided by the remains of potteries dating from this time which have been found in the forest—Alice Holt—south of the village.

Parish registers indicate that Bentley boasted what must have been a forerunner of today's technical colleges—a "school of industry" for local child workers. In the year 1796 they produced 2,197 pairs of yarn gloves and 60 pairs of worsted. They were paid 4d a pair.

Twenty years earlier a parish meeting had resolved not to provide relief for anyone who drank or frequented public houses—an ironic decision in view of the enormous contribution to the brewing industry made by local farmers, whose hopfields in later years won many gold medals for their owners in trade exhibitions.

# Bentworth 🦢

A French connection which started at the time of the Conquest and survived the Hundred Years War, the Reformation, and the Napoleonic era was celebrated at Bentworth in 1978. The Normans granted the Manor to the Diocese of Rouen, and before long Bishop Odin Rigaud visited his English acquisition. At an anniversary service 600 years later a welcome guest was his successor, Monseigneur André Pailleur, 110th Bishop of Rouen.

In the interval, however, a certain amount of ecclesiastical ill-will was discernible. At the Dissolution of the Monasteries Abbot Stevens, deposed from his comfortable occupancy of Beaulieu, was given the living of Bentworth and he ejected the incumbent. This was a blind man called Palmes, who had infuriated his bishop by his over-enthusiastic support for Protestantism (it included getting himself married). Stevens' supporters broke into the parsonage, barricaded the tithe barn, and "hired men to jangle and ring the bells above all measure and custom of charitable induction".

The poet George Wither ("Shall I wasting in despair Die because a woman's fair? If she think not well of me, What care I how fair she be?") was born at Bentworth in 1588 and often expressed a wish to return to its "beechy shadows" before his death. But he died in what he called "steaming London" at the age of 79 and was buried in the Savoy Chapel.

# Binsted 🦢

Binsted Rock is neither a dance nor a peppermint-stick with the name of the village all the way through. It is a local stone, and among the buildings for which it has been used are Victorian extensions to Binsted Wyck Place. Built around a 16th-century farmhouse, but with the remains of a Roman villa somewhere underneath the lawns, it was bought by William Wickham, Chief Secretary for Ireland, on his retirement in 1811. In 1892 his grandson—also William—became Conservative MP for East Hampshire on defeating the Liberal candidate, John Bonham Carter. But his grand-daughter

Charlotte married Sir Edgar Bonham Carter, and it was she—in her own words, "a compulsive gardener"—who first opened the beautiful gardens of Binsted Wyck to the public.

Telegraph House at Binsted was built as a link in the semaphore chain set up during the Napoleonic Wars to connect the Admiralty in London with the fleet at Portsmouth. In 1973 a firm wanted to demolish the tall white signal-station and replace it with a house, but it was listed as a building of special interest and permission to renovate it properly was granted to a private owner.

Old Palace
Bishops Waltham

# Bishop's Waltham

The original bishop was Henry of Blois, brother of King Stephen. He built his palace of flint, but the fortifications proved inadequate 500 years later when 200 of the King's Men were besieged by Parliamentary troops during the Civil War. Bishop Curle himself escaped only by hiding in a manure cart! Cromwell ordered the palace, in the descriptive technical term of the day, to be "slighted"—the flint proved a useful building material for local people.

Between Blois and Curle the palace saw the death of a bishop more famous than either, William of Wykeham.

23

Royalty was entertained on various occasions. In 1522 a "Treaty of Bishop's Waltham" was signed between Henry VIII and Charles of Spain.

The ecclesiastical holdings included a deer-park surrounded by a double-ditched bank, the "lug" (boundary), and also Waltham Chase, in which deer might be hunted only by the bishop and his men. However, episcopal rights were abandoned in the 18th century after it had become notorious for the activities of the Waltham Blacks, who may have been gentlemen-poachers in origin but degenerated into a lawless mob who had to be put down by special legislation.

French prisoners-of-war kept at Bishop's Waltham during the Napoleonic Wars included Admiral Villeneuve; he was billeted at the Crown. Even his men seem to have enjoyed some degree of freedom (see Odiham), being allowed to walk as far as "Frenchman's Bridge"—though one was shot dead when he failed to respond to a sentry's challenge.

In 1822 the Reverend Henry Veck published a book of hymns for use in the parish. His music was revived in 1976, when clergy robed in Victorian style conducted a service at which musicians played on contemporary church-band instruments, including the concertina and crumhorn. A successor of Mr Veck's claimed that "the history of Waltham is that of the great, the wise and the good". Charitably he ignored not only the Waltham Blacks but such occasional sinners as the man whose gravestone bears a crosscut saw to commemorate the fact that he fell dead while sawing on a Sunday.

Bishop's Waltham's 19th-century prosperity was reflected in the founding in 1809 of a local bank. Four generations of the Gunner family ran it, at one period issuing their own banknotes; and for its last 25 years, before being sold to Barclays in 1953, it was the only remaining private bank of its kind in the country.

To a large extent Gunner's was a farmers' bank: but long before its foundation the market at Bishop's Waltham prompted the indignant comment from the citizenry of Winchester that it flourished "to the great detriment of the citie".

Local industries once included candle-making. When the factory closed, the cast-iron vats used for melted wax were carted out into the fields and used as cattle-troughs. And for

100 years there was a flourishing brickworks the products of which were used in the construction of Blackfriars Bridge in London and the Suez Canal. It specialised also in various articles of terra-cotta, including jugs, vases, and candlesticks. The Blanchard family, who owned it for much of its existence, were, however, particularly proud of their balustraded staircases. There exists a photograph dating from the 1890s showing Mr Mark Blanchard, top-hatted, black-suited, and impressively-whiskered, standing on a demonstration staircase in a temporary building which was deliberately fired so that three men could demonstrate that—like Shadrach, Mishak, and Abednego—they had enough faith to be fireproof. What a superb piece of film it would have made for a television advertisement! The firm was eventually bought up by a Southampton firm which closed it down in 1957.

One scheme which never materialised at all, though it did receive parliamentary approval, was for a River Hamble navigation reaching as far as Bishop's Waltham. The railway did arrive, in the form of a branch from the main line at Botley, in 1863. It carried its last passengers in 1933 and was finally closed to goods as well in 1968. The station had been sited, with maximum inconvenience, immediately beyond a level crossing—but there had once been a plan to continue the line northward to Ropley and/or Petersfield.

In this century the village has seen its gas and water undertakings sold to Gosport companies, the closure of its county court and grammar school, the disapparance of its rural council, and the "demotion" of its Crown post-office to a sub-post-office. In recent years the tempo has quickened again, though not to the point where 16 pubs flourish once more, or young "sportsmen" ride at full tilt up the High Street trying to lasso the figure of the traditional black boy outside the tobacconists. The "black boy" was a variation of the American "cigar store Indian" who stands outside a shop to indicate that it sells tobacco. Wearing a crown and kilt of metal fashioned into the shape of tobacco leaves, Waltham's three-foot black boy stood above the Country Stores for several generations and was repainted in red, white, and blue for George V's silver jubilee. Six years ago he was replaced by a replica in glass-fibre, the original having ended up in somebody's garden—perhaps when the shop stopped selling tobacco—as a sort of up-market gnome.

# Bishopstoke 🦊

A map of 1872 shows the London and South Western Railway driving almost due south as the River Itchen and the Itchen Navigation loop through the water-meadows. Branch lines to the east and west meet at a station called Bishopstoke Junction, where 20 years previously a county cheese market had been established to take advantage of an important new centre of communications.

Between the station and the village on the map are Barton Farm and Barton Mill. "Barton" is the name given to a single terrace of houses, with the Crown at its northern end, on the opposite side of the main line where Dew Lane leads to two farms, Great and Little Eastley. This was the future railway town of Eastleigh just over a century ago!

But back to the Itchen and the Navigation. In 1838 Robert Mudie had noted: "The church and the village are beautifully situated, the former close by the bank of the river, with which the barge-course forms an inosculation a little above, but they part again at this point." Inosculation means "the passing of one thing into another". Mudie was displeased to note among older buildings "one plain modern box among the trees across the millpond" and, between it and the church, "another in true pastry-cook style". But another writer recorded in 1908 that "many modern red-brick cottages are now in process of building at both ends of the village to supply the needs of the men who are employed in the Eastleigh Railway Works, which are rapidly increasing in size". This refers to a decision to move down the carriage-works from what had been the LSWR's original London terminus at Nine Elms.

A 19th-century rector of Bishopstoke, Dr Thomas Garnier, enlarged the rectory garden and planted in it trees from all over the world. He was commemorated in Winchester Cathedral by a medallion portrait made from a miniature by Richard Cockle Lucas (see Chilworth). The doctor's niece, Lady Newdigate, considered it too severe and the Dean gave permission for a second sculptor to provide it with "the benignant kindly expression he had always had in life".

Garnier's successor was the Reverend Robert Harrison. He had married the daughter of another parson, Mr Knight of Steventon—son of Jane Austen's brother Edward (who changed his name on inheriting a fortune from a distant cousin). Robert's son William recalled that the tower of the church, built in 1825, was not strong enough for the bells to be properly rung. However, one was regularly "chimed" by the parish clerk, an old man with a top-hat and a stick, every Sunday morning at 8 o'clock "though there was no service at that hour nor ever had been I suppose in the memory of man". The bells were installed in the present church, which was opened in 1891. For years the tower was all that remained of the old one.

There is a nice quotation from a contribution by Miss C. M. Yonge—her Uncle George, a cousin of the novelist Charlotte Yonge (see Otterbourne), lived at Stoke Lodge from 1866–1904—to *Bygone Bishopstoke*, a compilation by Dorothy Escombe: "A good number of Bishopstoke names must now be forgotten, from the closing of the old churchyard and its overgrown and neglected state."

This neglect provided local newspapers with what journalists call a running story for some 20 or 30 years. I remember writing a news item about the day they finally decided to clear it up. It was printed under the headline "Great energy in a country churchyard".

In 1858 Admiral Sir Henry Keppel bought "The Cottage", a building on the river bank with a garden on the site of an old tanyard, together with "some good Italian furniture" for £1,500. Five years later he wrote in his diary: "From my little preserve on the Itchen, Frank Rutland stocked the rivers in Tasmania with trout, which has proved very successful."

# Boldre 🦡

"Exposed to every temptation of pillage and robbery from their proximity to the deer, the game and the fuel of the Forest, these poor people were little better than a horde of *banditti*;

and without the opportunity of the humblest education or the benefit of decent example, presented a picture of savage life which perhaps was hardly parallelled in a civilised country."

That was how the Reverend William Gilpin saw his parishioners when he came to Boldre. An exceptional man, he was able and willing—determined, in fact—to do something about it. The foremost travel writer of his day, he devoted to his parish much of the proceeds of his best-sellers. The idea of landscape being something worth looking at was new to his readers, but they took avidly to such works as *Forest Scenery* and even enjoyed the slightly didactic tone of a man who had been for many years a schoolmaster. It was in fact a former pupil, the historian Mitford, who gave him the living at Boldre. He promptly set about improving the lot of his parishioners by reorganising the poorhouse and establishing a village school. Parson for 30 years, he died in 1804 and his own epitaph records that he and his wife lie "secured from the afflictions, and the even more dangerous enjoyments, of life. . . . It will be a new joy to meet several of their good neighbours who now lie scattered in these sacred precincts."

Poaching was not the only temptation for the people of the parish, which originally stretched right across the southern part of the New Forest with a chapel at Brockenhurst as a sort of ecclesiastical outpost. Smuggling was rife in Hampshire and many a village—Boldre is no exception—has stories of horses "borrowed" from their stables overnight and returned the next morning exhausted, but with a cask of brandy by way of hire. The county has many lanes (not to mention pubs, cafés, and private houses) with "Smugglers" incorporated in their names, and there is no doubt that what was a couple of centuries ago a wild coastline with unguarded ravines, known locally as bunnies or chines, offered many handy landing-places for contraband. A special Preventive Officer was posted to the parish at Pitt's Deep opposite an inn which the artist Thomas Rowlandson had particularly commended, when sketching it, for the excellence of its brandy.

In 1924 Eric Jones-Evans, then a village doctor (see Fawley) collected a version of the traditional Mummers' Play presented at Boldre. The mummers were bands of men and boys who took part in what may originally have been a resurrection myth—even in the most debased version a champion is always killed by an enemy and revived by a doctor. In the 18th and 19th centuries many English villages boasted mummers who went round from house to house with a short play in crudely rhyming couplets which by then seemed to include a folk-memory of the Crusades. There was often a Saladin and always a Turkish Knight, though often after generations of oral handing-on he became a turkey snipe. In times of agricultural depression farmworkers found it an important method of raising a few extra shillings just before Christmas, and another character was usually Little Johnny Jack who begged money from the audience (see Broughton, Bursledon, Otterbourne, Yateley, etc.).

Mr Jones-Evans not only took part in the revival of the Boldre Mummers' Play he collected, but acted the doctor part 50 years later when it was presented by Dave Williams and fellow folk-enthusiasts in local pubs and on television.

Another old tradition which survived in the village within living memory was the celebration of Oakapple Day. Children not wearing sprigs of oak or oakapples were greeted with cries of "Shickshacks!". An unusual local variation was that at midday the correct decoration was an ash-spray and the term of derision was "Monkeypowder"! Numerous happy coincidences have occurred during the compilation of this book; one of them is that on the day I wrote the first draft of this entry "Shickshacks" was one of the mystery words in the television parlour-game "Call My Bluff". The second draft was typed on May 29ᵗh—Oakapple Day.

Parish registers show that in 1671 Henry Baker went out shooting on the Lord's Day, and was killed when his gun went off accidentally: and that when two weddings were solemnised on the same day in 1791, one bridegroom refused point-blank to pay the king's tax, but that the other said if his wife was worth marrying at all she was worth the extra threepence. So he paid up for both of them.

Surnames appearing in the registers include Godsgrace, Tivito—some connection with the hamlet of Tiptoe, perhaps—and Weyenwrighter (Wainwright?). Among girls' names were Elriathen, who sounds like a character from "Lord of the Rings", and Rodygun—possibly a variation of Rade-gonde.

A church-door key is said to have come from Beaulieu Abbey at the time of the Dissolution. Music in church was at various times provided by a band. One instrument was a 14-hole bassoon played by Jesse Jenvey, whose family were wheelwrights in the village for 200 years. There was also a barrel-organ, with three tunes (two hymns, one of which was The Old Hundredth, and a psalm).

Robert Southey, poet laureate, was married at Boldre in 1839 to Caroline Bowes of Buckland nearby. She was his second wife: they had corresponded for 30 years, but his mental and physical health was already deteriorating. They lived at Buckland for three weeks, and after his death at his old home at Keswick three years later she returned to Boldre.

Intermittent demands for the establishment of a New Forest museum were voiced again in 1972 when a man who had found a 2,000-year old pre-Christian stone head in his cottage garden at Boldre lent it to a museum at Winchester—but then took it with him to his new home in Scotland.

# Botley

Although plans to make a navigable channel as far as Bishop's Waltham never materialised, Botley was at one time a modest inland port, with loaded barges coming up the River Hamble as far as the bridge below Botley Mill. This is the only Hampshire mill out of several hundred listed in the Domesday Book where flour is still ground—a factor recorded today on its flourbags. Although a turbine and a computer are now used in the production of many kinds of animal food, the demand from small bakers and housewives for stone-ground flour increased during the 'seventies "contrary to the company's expectations".

Botley was described by its most famous resident, William Cobbett, as "the most delightful village in the world". He came to Botley House in 1804 and bought Fairthorn Farm in 1807. The novelist Mary Russell Mitford thought the broad belt of trees he planted round it evidence of his good taste. His zeal for parliamentary and agricultural reform was appreciated less in high quarters, and resulted in a prison sentence. On his return from prison in 1812 the people of Botley—some believed he was so clever he could write with both hands simultaneously while talking about something else—took the horses from his postchaise and dragged him in triumph through the village.

A royal grant for a market at Botley goes back to 1267. A corn market was opened in 1829 and a cattle market the following year. The Market Hall was built in 1848, partly from public subscription and partly through Botley Farmers' Club. This had been founded by William Cobbett and his friend James Warner, who bought the manor farm in 1833.

Some 150 years later Hampshire County Council announced a scheme to make it the nucleus of an agricultural museum and countryside park stretching down the River Hamble and incorporating the old Norman church (the greater part of which was used in 1835 for the construction of a new church nearer the centre of the village). In 1979 the parish council and other bodies and individuals claimed that the county had ignored local opinion. After strenuous objections from those who feared a tourist invasion, preferred a natural countryside to an organised leisure area, and thought the whole thing a waste of money, a scaled-down plan was produced.

In coaching days Botley was the first stage east of Southampton. It had 14 inns and three posting houses—the Dolphin, the Bugle, and the Catherine Wheel. Here in the mid-18th century a party of revellers pulled up one of their company for falling behind in his drinking—literally pulled him up, on a rope going up to the bacon-rack of the inn kitchen. They then rushed out to watch some soldiers marching by but returned too late to "the man with whom they thought they had had some fun but whom, unintentionally, they had deprived of life". The Catherine Wheel—it figures in a parish register of 1670 and may have been the first inn in the village—became in 1882 the headquarters of the local temperance organisation. It was used during the first half of this century by a charitable organisation; and then became a shop and café.

There was another, less serious, bad joke in 1899 when a hoaxer publicised the forthcoming wedding of James Kent, son of a local farmer, and Miss Colman whose father was landlord of the Dolphin. Posters announced that all those who attended the ceremony would be given a new shilling—but they did at least appeal for "no unseemly scenes". Neither of the happy couple's fathers was amused.

Village industries at Botley included a cooperage, run by the Guillaume family, behind the Three Horseshoes (later a garage). They had a shed at Horsepool where ash saplings were steamed and bent into hoops for the barrels. They also used hazel and willow cut in Wildgrounds, Gould and Dock Copses, and along the road to Hoe Moor. The hoops they made were sent all over the country for use in making barrels for everything from pilchards to gunpowder. Production ceased during the First World War, though hurdle-making continued.

Market gardening became big business this century, though subject to inevitable changes. In 1947 a newspaper commented that: "Since cars became common, a new practice of selling superfluous stock by the roadside had tended to supersede the older plan of charging 6d for admission to a field on the understanding that one stayed as long as one could." Since then of course there has been a return to the pick-it-yourself principle—with no entrance fee, but a pair of scales to fix the cost of the operation at so much per pound . . . or kilo!

# Braishfield ✺

On one of the slopes which sweep up from the network of lanes, where new houses are beginning to fill the gaps between the thatched cottages, is what may be the oldest dwelling in England. The mesolithic household—it goes back some 8,500 years—was discovered in 1971 by a member of the Ordnance Survey staff, Mr Michael O'Malley. A keen archaeologist in his spare time—he's retired now—he unearthed a series of flints which led him to the discovery of a sunken hut. His work won him second prize in the BBC awards made in 1979 in connection with the television series "Chronicle".

Flint-knapping—breaking flintstones, originally for use as axe or arrow heads—is one of the traditional crafts demonstrated in the country fair which has been a feature of village life in Braishfield in recent years. Broomsquires, blacksmiths, thatchers, and wheelwrights have also shown their skills. A strictly 20th-century activity also featured has been lifting car tyres. A farmworker, 19-stone Gary Windebank, earned himself a place in the *Guinness Book of Records* by getting 60 off the ground—a total he later increased to 76.

Apparitions recorded in Braishfield include an Edwardian lady said to be looking for her lost jewels; and a human form that was occasionally seen in the branches of an old yew by a deserted farmhouse. In 1978 a householder recorded two varieties of "haunting"—one affecting the ears, the other the nose. She related how for some months after an elderly neighbour had died, footsteps were heard in the lane at about the time when he used to return from his nightly visit to the pub: and how her cottage was occasionally filled with the smell of baking which seemed to emanate from a recess (presumably an old bread oven) discovered during building operations.

# Bramley

"The church is small, simple, decaying, almost ruinous", wrote Mary Russell Mitford in the middle of the last century. Now visitors come from quite a distance to admire its flint chancel and brick tower, its 18th-century monument to Bernard Brocas and—a remarkable survival—its 16th-century pews. Miss Mitford may have been influenced by the fact that the village wasn't in particularly good shape, either, in her day—with the nearest passable road a mile away and the best route from one country house to another across the fields.

An 18th-century Vicar of Bramley, the Reverend Thomas Shaw, earned himself a rare seal of approval from Edward Gibbon. A footnote in *The Decline and Fall of the Roman Empire*, in which comments on the clergy tend to be entertaining but acid, says that Shaw was an honourable exception to "blind travellers [who] seldom possess any previous knowledge of the countries which they visit". At Bramley the vicar may have had the reputation of a Baron Munchausen with his traveller's tales: but he had journeyed all over the Mediterranean and was at one time resident chaplain to an English factory in Algiers.

# Bramshott (see also Liphook) ✒

In 1809 the Reverend John Monkhouse took over Bramshott parish, which includes Liphook and Passfield, from an absentee rector. Three years later he wrote: "The want of honesty, and the want of chastity, are the prevailing defects here." His parish registers record a succession of women whose occupation was given as "whore". We cannot entirely blame those said to have derived a steady income from sailors on the road to Portsmouth since the father of one illegitimate child was the rector's clerk.

Between 1810–20 there were 72 marriages of which Monkhouse commented "not less than 69 brides have been unchaste before marriage. Those who gain husbands are more fortunate than those who bear bastards but not more virtuous." In his will he left £1,850 for the education of the parish children except for those whose parents were given to "whoring, thieving, cheating, tricking, backbiting, over-reaching, and extorting".

With so much heavy sinning going on it's a wonder anyone in Bramshott found time for work, but the parish has an industrial record which goes back to the days of the Romans. The iron they worked had not run out by medieval times, which resulted in such memorable names as Hammer Bottom (neither a condition nor an activity but a place) and Henry atte Cinderheap—half a mile away and he might have been Henry Atte Wood or Attwood.

Wood provided charcoal for the 16th- and 17th-century foundries and power came from water. Labour may have included "guest-workers", for church registers of the period refer to "strangers at the Hammer". Did they come from the other side of the Channel or merely from a neighbouring parish? Damming up the Downwater was done at the orders of the Lord of the Manor to provide the foundry reservoirs known as Wakeners'—later Waggoners'—wells.

The manor building, largely unaltered since the 15th century, is believed to be the oldest continuously inhabited house in Hampshire, though the War Office became Lord of the Manor in 1917, when the first of a series of Army camps was erected in the parish. Various common rights have survived— 25 families still have the right (seldom exercised) to pasture geese on the common, where also the right to gather fuel is preserved under the name of "black smutting and white stumping". Roger Newman enlarges on this in his book *A Hampshire Parish*. During his researches he unearthed no less than 40 spellings of the name of the village including Branbresete (11th century), Bremblesathe (13th) and Bramshear (16th).

As well as ironworks, the parish we now know as Bramshott—"bramble" seems the most likely derivation—has seen paper-making, forestry and associated crafts, and milling. The oldest mill surviving at the turn of the century, dating back to 1750, belonged to Theodore McKenna, brother of the Chancellor of the Exchequer: Mr Newman records that it was burned down by suffragettes.

Less impulsive supporters of the rights of both men and women were the founders of the Fabian Society, Sydney and Beatrice Webb, who left the house they had built—Passfield Corners—to the London School of Economics. He was created Lord Passfield in 1929: she insisted on remaining Mrs Webb.

_Breamore Mill_

# Breamore 🌿

Though it has come to be pronounced Bremmer it was originally broom-moor. Among its mysteries is the Mizmaze, an intricate pattern cut in downland chalk 30 yards across. It dates from prehistoric times, though monks from Breamore Priory are said to have traversed it on their knees by way of penance. Evidence of a later form of punishment survives in the stocks placed, possibly as an object lesson, outside the old village school. The church is older than the long-demolished priory and was built some 80 years before the Norman Conquest. An inscription over an arch survives in the original Anglo-Saxon. In modern English it means, "Here is manifested the covenant to thee."

A corn mill at Breamore stopped operations—perhaps "ground to a halt" is for once the right phrase—in 1970 after some 400 years, with the retirement of Stanley and Geoffrey Hall, by then both around the 70 mark. They were, they said, no longer able to compete with the mass production of cattle feed. The traditional water-wheel had been replaced by a turbine at the turn of the century, but in their father's day just after the First World War the head miller had five millers and several waggoners working under him. Corn was brought to Breamore both by road and rail: but the line between Salisbury and West Moors was axed by Dr Beeching in 1964.

Other forms of transport survive at a countryside museum (where farm vehicles and machinery include a six-sailed reaper) in the 17th-century stables of Breamore House, an Elizabethan mansion largely rebuilt after a fire in 1856.

In 1979 the chairman of the Ringwood and Fordingbridge Footpath Society pointed out that not a single footpath or bridleway in the parish of Breamore was signposted. Perhaps the opportunity will arise for a sign indicating a walkway northward along the old railway track, which runs through a beautiful stretch of the Avon water-meadows before joining the Salisbury–Southampton line over the Wiltshire border at Alderbury.

# Brockenhurst 🌿

Probably brocks (badgers) and bracken had less to do with the name of the place than a Saxon called Broca. And Grigg Lane, once as twisty as a grig (a dialect word for a small snake or eel) has been somewhat straightened. When the railway from Southampton to Dorchester—known after its solicitor-promoter as Castleman's Corkscrew—came snaking through the New Forest in 1847, the old settlement where W. H. Hudson stayed while writing *Hampshire Days* embarked on a still-continuing process of expansion. By 1978 this had brought the population to 3,500—a figure more than doubled by the number of summer campers. That year, however, the station was declared the best kept in the Southampton area of the Southern Region.

Of course it had a head start—several heads, in fact—in the form of a series of photographs in the waiting-room by the spirited pioneer photographer Julia Margaret Cameron. She lived near Tennyson on the Isle of Wight and bullied him—not to mention Darwin, Longfellow, and Browning—into sitting for her. Passing tradesmen were also liable to be inveigled into posing. She tended to give startled porters copies of her photographic portraits by way of tips, and the Brockenhurst Station Collection commemorated the fact that it was here she met her son in 1878 after his long absence abroad.

The parish registers show that in 1670 one Henry Browne was fined, and had his horse and cart confiscated, for cutting down a tree to make a maypole. He complained in vain that the case had been "fomented by fanatics who have a prejudice to all customs used time out of mind". They had objected to his erecting a maypole rather than to his felling a tree: a reminder of Macaulay's comment that the Puritans hated bear-baiting "not because it gave pain to the bear but because it gave pleasure to the spectators".

Brokenhurst—not Brockenhurst—Park was built in 1769 by Edward Morant, a West Indies plantation owner who became MP for Lymington. The family finally moved out in 1958 after trying to run the 17-bedroomed mansion without servants for ten years. In 1812 Lady Caroline Morant started a Dame School there, providing the material for uniforms which the girls made up themselves. The "dame" was an 18-year-old girl Lady Caroline imported from London, Miss Ash. She was lame, and travelled about in a kind of wheeled chair drawn by a donkey. For the annual school treat in the Park the donkey wore white cotton trousers with ribbons in the Morant colours—blue and yellow. The family name is commemorated in a local pub, the Morant Arms. The Morant Hall, now demolished, was built in 1911. It was the scene somewhat later of the only Hunt Ball I ever attended.

New Park Farm, the site of the annual New Forest Show and the biggest farm in the forest, has been the scene of several agricultural experiments. During the Napoleonic Wars the traditional ingredients used in rope-making—chiefly sisal—were in short supply and crops of the plant known as Russian comfrey were grown as a possible alternative for use in the manufacture of naval rigging. The plant still grows here and there.

For long after the First World War, the plough turned up shoes from the mules of various units encamped at New Park. In the churchyard of St Nicholas are buried over 100 New Zealanders of the Seventh Division who had been brought to army hospitals at Balmer Lawn and Tile Barn Hill. Indian soldiers were cremated on a funeral pyre at Collier's Copse.

# Broughton 🌿

The Roman road from Sarum to Winchester runs along the ridge south of Broughton. In 1783 a pig of lead dating from the reign of the Emperor Nero was found in the village (having perhaps fallen off the back of a baggage-waggon). Two feet long and 156 lb in weight, it ended up in the British Museum.

A hundred years later a skeleton was found on Broughton Hill with the remains of a sword and the boss of a Saxon shield. Perhaps what he had needed was a resuscitating draught of elecampane—or alicampane as it was called in the Broughton version of the Mummers' Play (see Boldre), which has a British warrior slain in battle but revived by a bottle of the stuff belonging to the Saladin.

In 1248 John Mansel was granted the right to hold a weekly market at his farm, Broughton Manor. Less usually, the rector was, in 1314, given an endowment in the form of a columbarium, or pigeon-house (keeping pigeons, a useful form of winter food, tended to be the prerogative of the squire or the bishop). Its successor is now a circular brick building with a conical roof, dating from the reign of William and Mary. It was put up in the churchyard, conveniently near the rectory.

Another unusual construction in Broughton is the wellhead, a 30-foot bore sunk in the High Street in 1921, after a severe drought, as a memorial to Lieutenant John Trude Fripp who had been killed in the First World War. Other wells had run dry—a double problem for villagers who made their own butter and kept it just below the surface of the water in their well. One of them was a woman whose son brought her original butter-making jar to a "hobbies evening" in Broughton in 1979.

Queenwood Farm, between Broughton and Tytherley, was the scene of an early experiment in community living on a basis of practical socialism. Robert Owen and his followers came to Queenwood in 1839 and built a grandiose community headquarters they named Harmony Hall. Though mainly industrial workers from the north, the pioneers, using various experimental systems of manuring and cultivating, made a success of the farm—somewhat to the irritation of local farmers and much to the alarm of the Establishment everywhere. Anxious that socialism should fail, Church and State kept a close watch on the behaviour of the colonists, who committed such outrages as walking back from a pub in Broughton with cries of "Queenwood Socialists for Ever!"

"For ever" was over-optimistic: dissension within the movement and (understandably perhaps) lack of capital meant that in 1845 the experiment was abandoned.

There was also, however, an experimental flavour to the type of education provided at the school which then took over the "Harmony Hall" premises. It pioneered the teaching of chemistry, philosophy, painting, music, and surveying as well as Classical languages. Its Quaker headmaster got into financial difficulties after a few years and it was during the 40-year reign of a later head that (in 1887) a pupil observed:

"Broughton is a very nice little village. . . . Until this year Mr Fisher's shop, which is also the post office, was the best but now the fellows have almost deserted it for Mr Hinwood's new shop, which is the finest building in Broughton." The writer found the local speech "not easy to understand", but discovered that "Gie I a lolly" meant "Give me a sweet". The village band, he recorded, "wear a regular uniform. At the beginning of term, when we have plenty of money, they come up to play at Queenwood."

A more regular caller was Mrs Glue, the Broughton cobbler's wife, who used to drive up to the college with the young gentlemen's boot repairs in a little cart drawn by two dogs.

The building originally known as Harmony Hall and later as Queenwood College ended up in 1895 as a poultry farm. The last headmaster, who had continued to live on the premises, died in the fire which destroyed them a few years later.

Buckler's Hard

# Buckler's Hard 🦪

Nelson's *Agamemnon* was built at Buckler's Hard, today a double row of 18th-century red-brick houses leading down to a bend in Beaulieu River. A shipyard was just about all that materialised of a grandiose plan by John, Duke of Montagu, to build a port rivalling Southampton. The Duke was Master-General of Ordnance, Master of the Great Wardrobe, and Governor General of the Isle of Wight—obviously he dearly loved a title, and he appointed himself Lord Proprietor and Captain-General of the Islands of St Lucia and St Vincent. Like his descendant, the present Lord Montagu of Beaulieu, he actually owned Beaulieu River and its miniature estuary. Since he also owned vast plantations in the West Indies the idea of a private port at which his own goods could be landed had obvious advantages. However, his grand schemes were formulated at a time before depredations by the French and insurrection by the native islanders took place and rendered them impossible.

The Master Builder, a hotel at the end of one red-brick row, was from 1706–1805 the home of shipbuilder Henry Adams. In his time, and that of his sons, 50 warships were launched from the yards. A former inn became in 1963 a maritime museum, an adjunct of the motor museum at Beaulieu upstream, and in 1971 a 76-berth yacht harbour was opened to accommodate the seasonal floating population.

# Burghclere

Burghclere was in one of the areas worst affected by the Black Death in 1348. The ecclesiastical landlords—the monks of Titchfield Abbey—could call on villagers to carry out set duties on the land the abbey owned, including so many days' ploughing; but the population was reduced so severely by plague that only a quarter of the work was done.

Though farming has remained the main occupation, the village is near enough to Newbury to have been affected by the ups and downs of a subsidiary activity, the wool trade. As well as cloth-making there was lime-burning, with ivy-covered traces of the old kilns remaining as reminders of a long-abandoned village industry.

Unusual names in Burghclere include Scouse's Corner, which suggests an immigrant from Liverpool, and Hockley's Hole. The watercress beds here never dried out until the death of the last member of the family which owned them: but later they were re-dug, re-stocked and revived.

Any visitor to Burghclere would do well to see the Sandham Memorial Chapel, named for a young officer killed in the First World War. Stanley Spencer worked on the famous murals for six years, drawing on his own memories of the fighting in Macedonia and using real people from his own Berkshire village of Cookham for the resurrection scenes. Few people nowadays would react the way Arthur Mee did when he wrote in the Hampshire volume of his *King's England* series just before the Second World War: "We should come to them, if we do come, willing to receive a shock from what is called stark naked realism, but is to us unlike anything we have ever seen or ever desire to see."

The murals are both ambitious and impressive, and are reputed to be the most important series of decorative paintings produced in England this century.

# Buriton 🌿

Petersfield was once, ecclesiastically, an offshoot of this village, with a chapelry administered by Old Buriton church. It has remained a village known to the world chiefly for its association with two men—a natural historian, and a historian on the grand scale.

Buried at Buriton is John Goodyer, the pioneer botanist who anticipated the work of both Linnaeus, halfway across the continent in Switzerland, and Gilbert White, in another corner of the county at Selborne. Goodyer noted and appraised not only familiar native plants but such comparative newcomers as the potato—and tobacco. His reputation was so high that during the Civil War a royalist general ordered all ranks "on all occasions to defend and protect John Goodyer, his house, servants, family, goods, chattels and estates of all sorts from all damages, disturbances and oppressions whatsoever".

In 1719 the grandfather of Edward Gibbon bought what the historian was to describe as "an old mansion in a state of decay". This was a timber-framed house, possibly of 15th-century origin, on to which a Georgian front had been grafted and other alterations made so that it was "converted into the fashion and convenience of a modern house; and if strangers had nothing to see, the inhabitants had nothing to desire. The spot was not happily chosen, at the end of the village and the bottom of a hill; but the aspect of the adjacent grounds was various and cheerful; the downs commanded a noble prospect; and the long hanging woods in sight of the house could not perhaps have been improved by art or expense."

The hill, the downs, and the woods are today appreciated not only by local people but by those who use the long-distance country walk which starts in a field above the church and continues by way of Chanctonbury Ring and Ditchling Beacon to where the South Downs curve into the Channel at Beachey Head.

# Burley 🦎

The people of Burley probably feel they have had a lot to put up with. There used to be the Bisterne Dragon, which came steaming down from Burley Beacon for a daily pint of milk; and now there are the hordes of visitors who make rather more extensive demands on a village much beloved by the operators of coach tours.

The dragon—perhaps the legend is based on a folk-memory of an outlaw or a wild boar—was eventually despatched by a volunteer from the village who rendered himself fireproof, or dragonproof, by smearing his clothes with sticky birdlime and then rolling in broken glass: but his hunting dogs were killed in the fray. The name Dragon Lane survives.

So, until the First World War or thereabouts, did the annual Scuggy Hunt—a sort of Boxing Day meet for the boys of Burley in which squirrels were caught and roasted on a bonfire to the accompaniment, it seems, of a good deal of rowdy drinking. Earlier, there had been a tradition in the village which ensured that all would be quiet when occasion demanded, as it did when cargoes of contraband passed by. There was even a living warning signal, literally a Red Alert, in the shape of Lucy Warne. She kept a lookout from the high ground toward Picket Post, and if she wore a scarlet cloak it was a sign that she had spotted the Revenue Men.

There were, however, more respectable ways of passing the time—making music with the village band, for instance. This was sufficiently well thought of to be invited to France in 1957 at a ceremony commemorating the 12th anniversary of the Dieppe Landings. But in 1968 its disappearance was cited by the chairman of the parish council as an instance of the way Burley was dying as a result of county council preservation policies allegedly leading to a shortage of people in their twenties and thirties. The number of schoolchildren was found to have halved; in 1970 the youth club closed, the membership

44

having dwindled to six; and in 1973 there was great difficulty encountered in finding anyone to play the back legs of a horse in the village pantomime.

But in 1979, after seven years in which the village lost seven shops, the secretary of the local Business Association claimed that the tide had turned. Certainly the birthrate was going up again. In 1968 only one baby had been born in the village but ten years later the parish councillors who had rashly voted to provide every baby with a Jubilee crown, a mug and a silver spoon were slightly taken aback to find the total of eligible infants was 11!

# Bursledon 🦢

The River Hamble was a positive invitation to invaders, and the North German tribes who gave their names to Anglo-Saxon civilisation established themselves on this part of the South Coast in time to fend off the next wave of incomers. Such defensive skirmishes have been elaborated into major naval engagements and we read how King Alfred's men sank 20 Danish longships at Brixedona: which almost reached the history books as a full-scale Battle of Bursledon, AD 877.

What looked like the strongest piece of evidence was a wreck uncovered in 1874. Hearing that "a private individual was removing timbers wholesale", the First Lord of the Admiralty—Lord Selborne—in 1880 "stopped the plundering for private gain". Hampshire Field Club inspected the remains with considerable interest in 1899, but within 30 years it had been embarrassingly identified by experts from the National Science Museum as "a large sailing ship of the mid-19th century". Perhaps she was one of the Danish windjammers which used to put in at Bursledon with corn for the mills upstream (see Botley): if so, legend at least got the nationality right!

With so many years as a busy port and shipbuilding centre behind them, Bursledon people themselves may have had their own suspicions about the "longship" story. In AD 700 St Boniface (né Winfrith) left from here for the Holy Land, though his major achievement seems to have been that, as Archbishop of Mainz, he organised Germany into bishoprics.

On St George's Day 1338 the warship *St George* was dedicated by the Bishop of Winchester and the Abbot of Netley. In the reign of Charles II, Daniel Defoe's early (and rather crabby) guidebook, *A Tour Through The Whole Island of Great Britain*, noted: "Here is a building yard for ships of war." But he used the information he gathered for his fiction, too, and the hero of his *Captain Singleton's* adventures sailed—aged 12—from Bursledon on his voyage to Newfoundland.

Several shipbuilders are commemorated on tombstones and plaques, among them Philemon Ewer, who died in 1750 having built "seven large ships of war for His Majesty's service during the late wars with France and Spain: an ingenious artist, an excellent workman, and an honest man".

Other local industries have included brewing, brickmaking (the products of the now defunct Bursledon Brick Company, with the firm's initials clearly incised, may puzzle archaeologists of the future), and ironworking. In 1977 an 18th-century map was found to show "Mr Gringo's furnice", confirming the shrewd suspicions of an industrial archaeologist who had spotted some likely-looking mounds 30 years earlier.

The works of a windmill erected during the last century at one of the highest points in the village were said in 1979 to be "the best preserved of their kind in Hampshire". The windmill last operated at about the turn of the century, but years later old people recalled the annual cavalcade to the mill after the first threshing of the season, with the carthorses wearing bells on their harness and scarlet rosettes.

Other old traditions which survived until the First World War at Bursledon were Garland Day ("the first of May/Is Garland Day—/A penny to see my garland!"), which included a church parade by the Free Foresters and a fair and feast on the village green; and the Mummers' Play (see Boldre). This was a short, debased version with "parts"—rather than named characters—a long way from their origins in the Crusades: "Oh you Turkey Snipe/Go home to your own lands to fight/ Tell the Americans what I've done/I've killed a thousand to your one."

A custom which grew up in Victorian times was pitching the heavy gate of the timber tollbridge into the river on New Year's

Eve. The bridge was built in 1875 by a company which also maintained the road through Park Gate to Bitterne. The county council bought the bridge in 1932 (the gate was taken to the Recreation Ground). Its successor dates from 1934 but has now lost through traffic to the motorway which crosses the Hamble a little way upstream.

**Calshot** (see **Fawley**) 🌿

# The Candovers 🌿

Philip Sheail has recorded in *A Downland Village* how in 1839 a traveller passing along the turnpike road which followed the course of the Candover Brook noted three "respectable gentlemen's houses"—North and South Hall, and Preston House. This last, by then some hundred years old, had originally belonged to William Guidott, a descendant of the Florentine Antonio Guidotti who in 1529 married the daughter of a Southampton merchant-mayor. The connection between the village and the port was revived in 1800 or thereabouts when a later owner of Preston House, John Blackburn, somehow acquired the clocktower of the Audit House at Southampton and had it re-erected over his stables.

This century has seen as many changes of ownership at Preston as the last. In 1961 it was bought from a member of the Courage brewing family for £331,000; sold in 1973 for £2 million to Peter Cadbury, whose business background included cocoa and television; and bought for £3 million in 1979 by John Sainsbury who, as they say, needs no introduction from me (come to think of it, I must have helped him pay for it).

I wonder if the new owner knows about a much earlier link between Preston Candover and the provision trade? The name Bangor Wood is now all that remains of a Welsh connection outlined by Shirley Toulson in *The Drovers' Roads of Wales*. From South Wales, cattle were for many centuries driven to markets in Surrey and Kent along ancient tracks of which one (see **Stockbridge**) passed Bangor Wood with a rest for watering at Bangor Inn, now demolished. "The County Council has even filled up its well", writes Ms Toulson. She records that it was once owned by two brothers—one of whom slit the other's throat to gain control of what was evidently a lucrative business. The story adds a sinister undertone to the notice which in later years announced:

> Stop in, young man, be not afeard,
> And for one penny I'll shave your beard—
> And you shall have for pennies nine
> Supper and bread and breakfast thine:

the purveyor of B&B was also a barber.

Mr Sheail's portrait of Preston Candover lists other trades practised in the village in the middle of the last century: there were two grocery shops (one was a bakery as well) and a butcher's; while craftsmen included shoemakers, blacksmiths, hurdlemakers, wheelwrights, a carpenter, a bricklayer, and a tailor. Its self-sufficiency is underlined by the fact that when the parish decided to build two cottages for poor families they were erected by local craftsmen with materials, including timber and bricks, supplied from local farms.

By this time nearly four-fifths of Preston Candover had been carved up (following the Enclosure Act) between three landowners—the Jervoises of Herriard Park, the Blackburns of Preston House, and Winchester College. The only common land remaining was at Oakhills, but this too was enclosed in 1870.

The hold of the Establishment over the lives of the village is exemplified by the fate of William and Maria Parker, who were among ten or twenty people converted to the Mormon faith in 1851 by a visiting American missionary. William lost his position as parish clerk and was sacked from the brickyard; his wife was dismissed from the position of village schoolteacher; and they were both evicted from their cottage.

"At Preston Candover", wrote William Cobbett, "there is an avenue of yew-trees, probably a mile long, each tree containing, as nearly as I can guess, from twelve to twenty feet of timber, which, as the reader knows, implies a tree of considerable size. They have probably been a century or two in growing." The trees are still there, with a notice saying "Private Road" at either end: but they're at Chilton Candover, connecting the old turnpike road (now the B3046) with the shorter alternative over the downs.

Fifty years ago some excitement was caused by the discovery at Chilton Candover of what was variously described as an underground church, a catacomb, and even a temple of Mithras (well, there's the site of a Roman villa not far away). An old parishioner had told the vicar how, when he was a boy, he and his mates would "go down under the church into a big hole and kick skulls about". Excavations revealed a crypt divided into two portions which corresponded exactly with the nave and chancel of a Norman church demolished in 1878.

# Chandler's Ford ❦

Was there ever a chandler, in the sense of a provision merchant or, in the earlier meaning of the word, a purveyor of candles? The most unlikely suggestion is a ship's chandler (presumably waylaying master mariners on their way to Southampton and offering to provision their ships!). For sheer ingenuity, however, the prize goes to the theory that the name comes from French émigrés who left Chalons and settled hereabouts to make the kind of worsted known as chalon or shalloon (see Whitchurch). More likely is that a man with the surname of Chandler owned land in the neighbourhood in medieval times. What we do know is that a hundred years ago there was not one ford but two.

King's Lane commemorates the route by which the charcoal-burner William Purkess brought the body of King William Rufus to Winchester from the spot where (accidentally or ritually) he was killed by an arrow-shot in the New Forest. Merrileas Road recalls the cherry-orchards which Richard Cromwell, the Protector's son, and his wife used to visit when they lived at Hursley Park (see Hursley). "Merries" is an old word (in French, merise) for cherries, and there was an annual "Merrie Feast" at Ramalley, still a local name. One theory says it's a corruption of Merrilea: another connects it with ramson, or wild garlic.

In Victorian times Mr Bull's brickworks at Chandler's Ford supplied bricks for the building of the Law Courts in London. Output was such that the schoolmaster complained his boys were "constantly up all night burning bricks, so that they are ill-fitted for being taught the next day".

In a survey made at about this time Barton-on-Sea and Chandler's Ford were nominated as the two healthiest places in Hampshire. In the latter, sanatoria were built among the pines and the workhouse was later converted for this purpose and renamed Leigh House. A developer called the village "an inland Bournemouth"; but even the most loyal Chandler's Forder would admit that his parish lacks more than a coastline to justify the comparison.

It was when the Hursley Estate was split up in 1892 that Chandler's Ford began to develop and a separate parish was carved out of Hursley, Otterbourne, and Stoneham. Establishing a village identity was never easy, partly because of the even more rapid growth of the neighbouring railway town down in the Itchen water-meadows. For some, its Big Brother attitude was typified by the erection of notices on the Winchester–Southampton road either side of Chandler's Ford saying "Welcome to Eastleigh".

*Jane Austen's House, Chawton.*

R.ea.

# Chawton ✎

One of the oldest buildings in the village used to be a forge: alas, this century it has been smithless. A neighbouring building is the redbrick cottage of which Jane Austen wrote:

> Our Chawton home, how much we find
> Already in it to our mind.

She and her mother and her sister Cassandra took it in 1809—Chawton House having been left to her brother 15 years previously. She wrote *Mansfield Park, Emma,* and *Persuasion* at Chawton, moving in 1816 to her last home at Winchester.

Until after the Second World War the house was divided into two dwellings, but it has now been restored into something very close to its condition in Jane's day.

Buried at Chawton is Sir Edward Bradford (born 1836), who served in India both during the Mutiny and afterwards—

"suppressing crime, introducing good government, and popularising railways". He lost an arm when attacked by a wounded tiger. At 53, he was appointed Commissioner of Police in London, and in that post he stopped a strike, restored discipline, and made the force "a model for the world".

# Cheriton 🦌

In 1976 members of the Sealed Knot Society, which enthusiastically re-fights the battles of the Civil War with the minimum of bloodshed and the maximum of television coverage, set up a memorial stone to the "Cheriton Fight" of 29th March, 1644. Until then, nothing had marked the decisive defeat of the King's Men under Lord Hopton by Sir William Waller's Parliamentarians.

There were something like ten thousand men on either side: but Waller was flushed with his success at Alton and Chichester while Hopton knew that many of his men were conscripts liable to desert. The main body of the Royalist cavalry charged but then "wheeled about to an unreasonable distance, and left their principal officers to shift for themselves". The horsemen, attacked by musketeers, wavered and were finally routed by the Roundhead cavalry. Hampshire's own unit, the Hambledon Boys led by Colonel Norton, charged the Cavaliers in the rear. The Kentish Regiment, fighting for Parliament, then attacked Royalist foot-soldiers: "the first of the King's Men that are said to have run away", says one account, "were two regiments of Irish". But before long most of Hopton's Hampshire levies had melted into the background leaving 2,000 firearms in ditches and hedges behind them.

Parliament lost perhaps 900 men, and the King 1,400. As one historian put it, the defeat was "no ordinary repulse. Not only had it put an end for ever to that scheme for the occupation of Kent and Sussex which, from the very beginning of the war, had played such a part in the Royalist strategy, but it set free the armies of the Earls of Essex and Manchester for offensive operations. Morally, the effect of the battle was even more decisive."

While Waller went on to capture Basing House and the walled city of Winchester—a suburb on high ground to the south is still called Oliver's Battery—the legends began to accumulate of lanes at Cheriton that ran with blood and of mass burials at Lamborough or Lamberry Field, on the high ground towards Hinton Ampner. The mound here was shown in 1930 to be a neolithic long barrow. A more reliable connection with the battle was a dwindling pile of stones at the bottom of Brockwood Hill which marked the grave of a cavalier's horse. More interestingly among the eye-witnesses of the three-hour battle was a man detailed to report on the achievements of Waller's London Brigade—an early war correspondent "imployed in the service of City and State".

As memories of the Cheriton Fight faded the inhabitants settled back to their traditional occupations of farming—and smuggling. During the ensuing couple of centuries squat bottles of Hollands Gin in local cottages were quoted by several writers as evidence of a thriving trade which relied on isolated farmhouses as storage and collection points for various kinds of contraband.

The source of the river Itchen is marked on Ordnance Survey maps a mile south of the village, through which it flows—providing, until recently, several cottages with their own water supply. The water came either as an open stream, or through a well in the garden, or even the kitchen. One old cottage, with a well deep and clear enough to supply neighbours when other sources dwindled, reported trouble in 1954 when the water came up tasting of paraffin.

Fortunately, there has long been an alternative for anyone wishing to quench his thirst: the village pub, which—as The H.H. rather than the Hampshire Hunt—claims to have the shortest name of any in the country. For many years the old pub game of Rings flourished here; and when it was revived in 1959 the players included "Turp" Brown, renowned throughout the county as an authentic folk-singer in the old tradition.

# Chilbolton ❧

The ghost is reputed to be that of a nun from the priory over the watermeadows (see Wherwell). She was brought to the house for some misdemeanour and then walled up. The house, when modernised, thus became one of a very small minority able to boast a Haunted Bathroom. She would keep looking out of the window, which one owner of the house (presumably after complaints from passers-by) consequently had blocked out. In modern times several guests have asked who was the mysterious figure in nurse's uniform.

Traditions have been slow to die in Chilbolton. There was Garland Day—here the version of the rhyme recited by children as they went from house to house was "Please to see a fine garland/Made early in the morning/The first of May is Garland Day/Please to see a fine garland "—and the baking of mid-Lent wafers. These wafers have been made for 200 years or so by the Baverstock family, who still live in the village. They are baked in special wafer-irons or tongs—circular plates, marked with the initials I.S. for Iesus Saviour, pivoted on long handles. Waffles and waffle-irons are a Dutch-American version of the same thing, though the batter used is obviously much richer than the austere mixture suitable for Lent!

The grindstone in the village street was bought with money left over from celebrating the coronation of King George V in 1910. Originally it was placed near the church and was regularly used by farmhands sharpening scythes and sickles. Later patrons included American servicemen with sheath-knives, which brings us to the construction of Chilbolton Airfield during the Second World War. When the war ended, thousands of Allied prisoners-of-war were flown here before dispersal to their units or homes. Later it was used by RAF officers training on new aircraft, including Vampire jets, after initial demonstrations by test pilots. Now it houses a radio observatory.

## Chilton Candover (see The Candovers) ❧

# Chilworth 🌿

The unusual name of the local pub, The Clump, derives from an ancient earthwork. A modern earthwork near by, the M27, now splits the village in two.

In 1809 the church was "without a ceiling, little better than a hovel, with a belfry like a pigeon-house"—a pity, because its 12th-century bells were among the oldest in the county. Fortunately, it was rescued from further decay in 1812 at the expense of the Lord of the Manor, whose lands were once connected to Southampton by a road running across what is now the Sports Centre and the Common. Maintaining it seems to have been quite a problem: in the 17th century one William Ffox was fined several times for digging clay from the highway.

The thatched post-office was originally built to house the squire's hounds, and was handed over for its present use in 1900 by Mr John Willis Fleming. His family name is perpetuated in a pub at Swaythling, the Fleming Arms, and by Fleming Park at Eastleigh.

Another unusual building, sadly demolished soon after the First World War, was "The Tower of the Winds". This was a Victorian Gothic extravaganza built by the sculptor Richard Cockle Lucas. Born in the first hour of the 19th century, he was the son of a Salisbury cloth-manufacturer. In old age he published a booklet recounting his boyhood adventures among the fairies he encountered in the old fulling mill and at Old Sarum. A familiar figure in the neighbourhood, he drove about standing in a sort of chariot and wearing a toga-like cloak. He was on friendly terms with Lord Palmerston at Broadlands and acquired an artistic reputation which enabled him to show his sculptures at the Great Exhibition of 1851, and resulted in a commission for a bust of Isaac Watts which still stands in Watts Park at Southampton.

He will, however, probably be remembered best by his wax bust of the goddess Flora. It was sold (along with "The Tower" and various other possessions) by Lucas's son, Albert Durer Lucas. It fetched a few shillings from a Southampton dealer but then worked its way up the artistic and financial ladder to Spinks in London. They passed it on to Mr Murray Marks, from whose Bond Street Gallery it was bought for the Kaiser

Friedrich Museum in Berlin by a German art expert, who attributed it to Leonardo da Vinci, for £9,250; an astonishing sum in 1909!

Occupants of a 17th-century timber-framed cottage at Chilworth have been subjected to an "aural" haunting. In 1972 Mrs G Macrae, whose family had occupied it for 200 years, recorded that they had found the experience amusing rather than frightening. The ghostly sounds include whispering on the landing, footsteps on the stairs, hands being washed: and, from outside, knocks on the door, rattles at the letter-box, and muffled crowd-noises.

# Corhampton 🦡

Corhampton Church is on one bank of the River Meon, Meonstoke Church on the other. When a stone coffin was dug up in a nearby field the bones were buried in Meonstoke churchyard and the coffin placed beside the door of Corhampton Church, where it stayed for 50 years. It somehow got broken, and the parochial church council thriftily stored its lead lining in the boiler-house awaiting a scrap merchant. A local resident who thought the whole thing should stay in the parish bought it, a bricklayer repaired it, and it has become a geranium bed—in the churchyard.

Inside the church, which was built in 1025, a series of medieval frescoes was covered by a cement wall some years ago when the sanctuary was rebuilt in red brick. Experts carefully uncovered them again in the sixties and found that one portrayed a miracle attributed to St Swithin when he restored a basket of eggs which an old woman had broken.

Corhampton was unlucky in its royal connections. In the 13th century Gilbert de Clare, Lord of the Manor, married the daughter of Edward I but when her husband died she secretly remarried. The King imprisoned the new spouse and, as it were, put him under house arrest. He was ordered to stay at Corhampton Manor until the de Clare heir came of age. Unfortunately, soon after doing so the heir was killed in battle.

Two hundred years later the Lord of the Manor, the Duke of Buckingham, came to a violent end while helping Henry VIII's agents in their inquiries into a plot against the King. Henry gave the manor to the Westons—one of whom was in due course beheaded on suspicion of having been a lover of Anne Boleyn.

Villagers are supposed to have burned down a cottage on Corhampton Down after the lady occupant had cursed a herd of cattle. She—or possibly another occupant—had the reputation of luring unsuspecting sailors bound from Gosport to London, whereupon they would be killed and robbed by her accomplices.

# Crawley 🐚

A story from Thackeray's *Vanity Fair*:

"It is related, with regard to the borough of Queen's Crawley, that Queen Elizabeth, in one of her progresses, stopping here for breakfast, was so delighted with some remarkably fine Hampshire beer which was then presented to her by the Crawley of the day (a handsome gentleman with a trim beard and a good leg) that she forthwith created Crawley a borough empowered to send two members to Parliament."

Though Crawley Court—now headquarters of the Independent Television Authority—had a "real" tennis court built for the pleasure of George IV when he was staying near by, the "old-world" appearance of the village is largely due to the imitation in modern times of traditional styles. To students of farming—and there are plenty of them about, with the Hampshire College of Agriculture a mile or two away at Sparsholt— the village is noteworthy for the still discernible 13th-century land pattern under which three great open fields were used for the rotation of crops.

# Crondall 🐚

It may have been the lesson learned from the blaze that destroyed the great tithe barn at Crondall which prompted a tradition of do-it-yourself firefighting efficiency. The barn, with three bays each large enough to accommodate two wagons loaded with grain, burned down in 1861. But 100 years later Hampshire County Council found the village was still relying on voluntary firemen, with an 18th-century hand-pump housed in a thatched wooden barn. The parish and rural district councils stoutly maintained it was an efficient unit, but the county—with Home Office support—pronounced it "costly and redundant". The area would, they decreed, in future be cared for by neighbouring forces. This claim brought a comment from the village that "they would let Crondall burn while Aldershot fiddles".

There used to be a Church House at the entrance to Crondall churchyard. There is a record of repairs sanctioned by the churchwardens in 1570, but it became derelict over the ensuing centuries—possibly because the traditional fund-raising activities known as Whitsun Ales were abandoned in 1643 with the arrival of Puritanism (incidentally the Parliamentary commander found Crondall "a hazardous outpost" before the fighting at Alton). The Church House, as an ivy-covered ruin, was finally demolished in 1878.

# Curdridge

Frog Mill, mentioned in a court roll of Queen Anne's reign, used to make paper for the *Morning Post*, long swallowed up by the *Daily Telegraph*. The mill, named after its one-time owner, a Mr Frogge, was pulled down about the end of the last century.

A stone which stood at various points in the village at different times bore a plaque announcing that it had been "erected to perpetuate a most cruel murder committed on the body of Thomas Webb, a poor inhabitant of Swanmore, on the 11th February, 1800". The remains of his murderer, a soldier, were "gibbetted on the adjoining common". The plaque was handed to Portsmouth Museum by Mr John Brickwood after its discovery in a pub belonging to his family brewery in that city. Another pub in the village, now a private house, had a landlord with two daughters: one married a Mr Batt, the other a Mr Ball. The pub was called The Cricketers.

One totally unlicensed operation from the history of Curdridge: in 1823 the Revenue Men seized a cart containing "tubs of spirits" passing through the village. Talking of spirits, a lady named Kate Hunt used to fly about Curdridge on a five-barred gate. As is often related in such cases, she had a witch's power to turn herself into a white hare and yes, when the hare was shot the witch's body was found with gunshot wounds! An unusual touch in Kate's case is that there was a whip-round to provide the silver for the special bullets essential in such armed witch-hunts.

# Damerham 🌿

Boundary revisions in 1895 took Damerham out of Wiltshire, though it is within a few miles of Salisbury, and placed it along with a couple of other parishes in Hampshire. This was part of a process of tidying up a border which, owing largely to the vagaries of ecclesiastical history, had been in a state of some confusion.

The village was within the confines of Cranborne Chase, where until 100 years ago the Lord of the Chase could claim rights of "vert and venison". This meant that anything providing food and shelter for deer, as well as the animals themselves, had to be preserved. An additional complication was that the village belonged to the Abbot of Glastonbury, which resulted in a good deal of bickering between ecclesiastical and civil authorities—represented in the 13th century by the Earls of Gloucester. There was more bickering when the Chase was divided: in 1616 the Pembrokes of Wilton sold Berwick St John and Damerham to the Cecils of Cranborne (another tidying up of boundaries).

After the Chase had been finally disenfranchised, farming and forestry developed along normal lines, though one occupant of Manor Farm, Tabitha Coffin, did have her little eccentricities. Anyone who annoyed her was given a ducking in the pond. Presumably she had some devoted and hefty henchmen to carry out the sentence.

Seasonal occupation included stripping trees of their bark, which was used in tanning: the operation was locally called rinding or rining.

There was also a sawpit. Long after it fell into disuse a ghostly white donkey which haunted the village used to trot along Steel's Lane and disappear where the pit had been.

# Denmead ✸

Denmead is a comparatively modern creation south-west of the original settlement. Barn Green, Hambledon, is what it used to be called. It became a parish on its own in 1880 and it was the first vicar, the Reverend Frederick Charles Green, who was largely responsible for giving it both a name and identity. Previously it had been a loose collection of scattered houses and cottages of which Black Horse Farm—later Little Denmead Farm—is probably the oldest. Much of the village was on the estate belonging to Ashling House, demolished in 1959. Among the most notable of many buildings to share the same fate over the past 50 years or so was the windmill which for about a century stood on the west side of what became Mill Road.

Like many villages in the hinterland of Portsmouth, Denmead started to expand when Portsea Island began to push its population up over Portsdown Hill. Terry Norman records in his pictorial history *Hambledon and Denmead* (Bay Tree, 1976) how Fred Tanner forged one of the first links between city and country with his bus fleet of red and silver "Denmead Queens". The last trip on 25th March, 1935, was made festooned with ribbons and carrying crates of free beer for the passengers. As the Queen drew into the Portsmouth terminus at North End an inspector could only comment "Make the most of it—tomorrow, you're Southdown!"

# Dibden ✸

The Manor of Dibden was divided into 23 lots and sold in 1813. For the previous 150 years the Lord of the Manor and his tenants seem to have spent much time and effort keeping a wary eye on each other's shortcomings. A Customs Book of the 17th century laid down that timber from the Lord's "waste" could be used for the maintenance of the church, his tenants' houses—and the village stocks. One particular responsibility seems to have been neglected. "The Lord ought to repair the pound", says one entry: and another, "the pound is wholly out of repair and useless". At different times various tenants were fined for cutting and selling peat, gathering furze, and neglecting fences and ditches. Later they invaded the manorial waste to dig clay, sand, and gravel.

The family of the song-writer Charles Dibdin (1745–1815) took its name from the village. He specialised in nautical themes both jolly ("Did you ever hear of Captain Wattle? He was all for Love and a little for the bottle") and sentimental, as in 'Tom Bowling': "Faithful below, he did his duty But now he's gone aloft."

Finally, a wonderful memory of village pleasures has fortunately come down to us through a report of the Dibden harvest festival celebrations of 1877. Following a glorious summer the church was filled with "a profusion of flowers and fruit, the freewill offerings of rich and poor throughout the parish, every gentleman's house, every farm and well-nigh every cottage contributing something to be presented as a thank-offering. After the service the labourers . . . headed by Beaulieu band proceeded to the large barn on Dibden farm where about 130 sat down to dinner. There was a cricket match (married v. single) in the afternoon."

# Dogmersfield ✺

The field by the lake where the waterlilies grow: a lyrical origin for a solid, even prosy, sounding name. Royal visitors in past centuries to the Bishop's Palace in Dogmersfield Park included Henry VI and Henry VII. One bishop, as a sort of royal secretary, helped to arrange the first meeting here of the latter's son Prince Arthur and his bride-to-be, Katherine of Aragon. The estate was among the properties acquired by Henry VIII's Chancellor Thomas Wriothesley, first Earl of Southampton (see Titchfield); his son replaced it with a Tudor mansion which the third Earl sold after a dispute with his tenants.

A new manor house—it became Dogmersfield College—

was built in 1728 by the first Baronet St John. His son Sir Henry enlarged it, demolished most of the existing village and made its green into Tundry Pond. He ensured that the Basingstoke Canal (see Greywell) made a detour round his park. The canal's promoters even had to build a special bridge to provide him with a new access to the house. The park itself was landscaped à la Capability Brown, and various artificial eyecatchers in the way of grottoes and follies were removed after less than half a century. An exception, possibly because it was on the "wrong" side of the canal, was a hunting lodge— now a private house—which survives with an elaborate triptych of a brick façade.

Sir Henry also rebuilt the village on lines so regular that a relative referred to it as his barracks. It was not until the 1830s that much notice was taken of any possible preference by the villagers for how and where they might like to live. Though Sir Henry's widow Jane had the four remaining cottages in the Home Park removed, a new settlement was built round the old hamlet of Pilcot. She appointed Charles Dyson as rector and he, with his friend John Keble (see Hursley) chose a site near by for a new church. She is also remembered for her annual gift of clothes to the daughters of estate workers; worn for the May Day celebrations, they consisted of blue-striped cotton frocks with white tippets and white straw bonnets with blue ribbons.

# Droxford ❧

The fact that the timing of the allied invasion of Europe in 1944 was decided on at Droxford must not blind us to an earlier claim to fame. It was the first place in England where the Jerusalem artichoke flourished . . .

This 17th-century success story was due to the fact that the pioneer botanist John Goodyer (see Buriton) spent some years here. A better-known figure associated with the village was Izaak Walton, who married the daughter of the rector, Dr Hawkins. It is not known whether the famous angler was attracted to the young lady first, or to the possibilities of fishing the Meon! A plaque recording his visits to the village was put up in the parish church in 1956.

Hawkins' predecessor, Nicholas Preston, was ejected by the Puritans, but returned to the living ten years later at the Restoration. In the first decade of this century the rector was Canon John Vaughan, who as a naturalist may in some means have carried on the village's botanical link started by John Goodyer.

The Meon Valley railway linking Alton and Fareham via Droxford was built by the London and South Western largely to block a Great Western scheme to continue its Reading-Basingstoke branch to Portsmouth. The *Railway Magazine* of June 1903 reported that the Meon Valley route had been "designed and constructed to form a portion of a main through line from London [via Aldershot, Farnham, etc.] to Gosport, Portsmouth, and Stokes Bay (for the Isle of Wight) and also Southampton via Netley". Its earthworks, bridges, and tunnels were wide enough for two tracks, and it was expected that the second would be laid within a few years: but road traffic grew, railway business dwindled, and the still-single line was closed in 1955.

When the railway-builders reached Droxford they unearthed bones, swords, spearheads, brooches, and shield-bosses—relics of a Jutish burial-ground. The Meon, like the Hamble and the Test, had proved a tempting route for invaders.

Invaders going the other way—members of the Allied Expeditionary Force which liberated Europe from the Nazis—had their headquarters at Droxford just before D-Day. In the late Spring of 1944 the stationmaster at Southampton was asked where in his area a train could stand unobtrusively for some days within the protection of a cutting. On 2nd June, a T9 4-4-0 Drummond locomotive steamed into Droxford with eight coaches in red LMS livery which made a startling change from the usual agricultural freight. Later they were supplemented by an LNER sleeping-car. The train and the station became the D-Day headquarters for Churchill, Eisenhower, Smuts, Mackenzie King, de Gaulle, Eden, and Bevin.

In 1966, ten years or so after the Beeching Axe had fallen, the track from Droxford to Wickham was used for trials of a 75-seater diesel railcar which it was hoped would bring new life to the Isle of Wight railway system and other moribund lines. In 1973, however, the victory of road over rail was underlined when permission was given for Droxford station and yard to be used as a training centre for drivers of heavy lorries.

Court House, East Meon—

R.C.G.

# East Meon

The highest village in the Meon Valley, it is where the River Meon rises—though with the sinking of deep boreholes in the chalk since the beginning of the century the stream-bed is often dry for its upper stretches.

The noble Norman church is the oldest building in the village: in the transept a stone marked "Amens Plenty" is believed to cover the grave of Parliamentary soldiers killed during the Civil War in a skirmish before the Battle of Cheriton (see Cheriton).

Two hundred years earlier, in 1441, following a great tempest "there fell a great multitude of rats" upon the malt-room at the vicarage. In the ensuing rat-hunt were discovered four

64

gold nobles and £20 in gold. The Crown claimed it, as the vicar, Thomas Wassaille, had not known it was there; but the King, Henry IV, ruled that he should be allowed to keep it because he had suffered great loss in the storm, five houses belonging to him having been blown down. It is not recorded whether this early instance of storm damage compensation resulted in anything being handed on to the vicar's homeless tenants.

East Meon's second oldest building is the medieval Court House. It was the Bishops of Winchester who held court here: but by the 20th century it was being used to house farm-workers, with the Great Hall as a cow byre. It was restored by an architect who bought it in 1927: the hall is used from time to time for theatrical performances by local players.

# East Tisted 🦢

Stories of longevity sometimes lack substance, but who can doubt that Isaac Bone, born at East Tisted in 1787, reached the age of 105? After all, he was sexton and parish clerk for 69 years—and celebrated his 100th birthday and his retirement on the same day by ringing three of the church bells together— one with each hand and the third with a foot.

For part of Bone's term as clerk, the vicar was the Reverend James Macaulay Cunningham, who figures in *Victorian Country Parsons* by Brenda Collins. His diary is full of such comments as: "Thursday January 2 1862: to Winchester for diocesan Board of Education. I went by train and found it a most expensive business, and as the meeting was utterly un-important I was vexed enough when I went."

Mr Cunningham had, after all, plenty to do in East Tisted. Visiting the sick was for him more than a mere formality: if necessary he would change their dressings as well. Nor was his care unappreciated, as another extract from his diary shows: "In evg. a v. pleasant tea-drinking at the school. It was got up entirely by the villagers—we had nothing to do with it, but were there only as guests. It was intended as an act of respect and regard by our people, and as such was v. pleasant. After tea

I made a short speech and they had some singing, the magic lantern, and ended up with a fire balloon."

In 1979 there were plans for extensive felling in Winchester wood, but a preservation order was placed on more than 300 trees in what was described as "an increasingly rare oakwood habitat". Human habitats at East Tisted have also come in for commendation: "Picturesque estate cottages, 1820 onwards" being listed in Gillian Darley's *Villages of Vision* as interesting examples of early estate planning.

# East Woodhay

Here the Welsh cattle-drovers (see Stockbridge) halted to have their herds shod with cleats—metal shoes which fitted over their hooves. This was as far as they could get along the green ox-droves before taking to the hard-surfaced roads to Newbury and beyond.

The village in fact has always looked to Berkshire. WI members of 50 years ago recalled how men and women would walk to Newbury after work for sacks of flour. And on Thursdays cans of barm (yeast froth) would be brought back and sold at twopence a can. So even in the 'thirties, long before sliced loaves in plastic wrapping, home-made bread was nostalgically rated higher than the shop variety!

Another memory is of frameworks for crinolines being made of brambles. The thorns were removed, the brambles left for 48 hours and then split in half lengthways to be bent into hoops. An old inhabitant of East Woodhay is recorded, in the WI's anthology *It Happened in Hampshire* as commenting that, "Some girls would have them very large—sometimes so big that they could hardly get through the carriage doors, and had to tilt them up sideways."

Hazel was of course one of the more conventional raw materials provided by the wooded slopes of the surrounding countryside. Hurdle-making from coppices was common, but there was also a sawpit dealing with heavy timber—among its products were railway sleepers for the London and South Western's "new" line from Basingstoke to Whitchurch, Andover, Salisbury and the West.

From 1891 to 1960 East Woodhay had its own station on the Didcot, Newbury, and Southampton line. Its promoters kept running out of money, and the original plan for connecting with the main line at Whitchurch, and building a terminus of its own at Southampton, never materialised. But for a time it made possible a day out at Winchester (the DNS station was called Cheesehill, later Chesil), and at the beginning of the century there was even a through train to Glasgow!

## Eastleigh (see Bishopstoke, Chandler's Ford) ⁖

# Easton ⁖

Much threatened recently by a plan to extend the M3, Easton is the country home of the author of the best-seller *Janet Marsh's Nature Diary*. Her father, a keen angler, had a fishing caravan—later a cottage—in this stretch of the Upper Itchen Valley: an area which, she says, has "held her spellbound" since her first sight of it as a 14-year-old schoolgirl.

"Easton Village", she writes, "is small, predominantly thatched, with the most beautiful church situated near the river. . . . Extensive areas of the river's flood-plain were converted to water-meadows in the first half of the 19th century: before that the Upper Itchen was considered unusable for watering because of underlying peat. The water-meadows were essentially a permanent and often elaborate irrigation system, formed into successive ridges and furrows. . . . With the loss of men knowledgeable in water-meadows management, known as 'drowners' or 'floaters', and the increasing cost of labour, the aqueducts and furrows fell into disuse." Traces of them are, however, clearly visible and many of the sluices are still operated.

Herbert Westfayling, says an inscription in the little Norman church, was "never betrayed into laughter". Commendation or criticism? He was one of five bishops who married the five daughters of a former nun called Agatha, who died in 1595 aged 90. Her son William Barlow was rector of Easton and they are both buried in the church. Agatha's husband—a former monk—was made a bishop by Henry VIII. Another of their sons-in-law, Toby Matthew, became Archbishop of Canterbury. He had a reputation as a wit; he must have found Herbert a disappointing audience.

# Eling 🐚

Totton, the cuckoo in Eling's nest, has an entry of its own: here we look at the settlement which grew up where the Bartley Water joins the estuary of the Test. The tide mill at the junction (descendant of one which figured in the Domesday Book) was written off by the Ministry of Local Government in 1961 as not even worth listing for historic or architectural interest. In 1975, however, the New Forest Council came to the rescue, starting a "buy-a-brick" campaign as restoration work began. The Department of the Environment chipped in with a grant of £7,500; and early in 1980 it was opened as a working museum.

The mill is on a causeway which incorporates the last toll-bridge operating in Hampshire, and for 600 years it helped to swell the finances of Winchester College. There was a hiatus—a 20 foot gap, in fact—in 1887 which cost the College £1,400 to repair: the Christmas mailcart to Marchwood just got clear before the water swirled up over the roadway. A temporary wooden footbridge was put up so that people could still get to Eling church from "the outlying district of Totton". Were they expected to pay a toll? As pedestrians, presumably not. The charge has always rankled, and not long ago the notion of mourners having to stop and pay tolls on the way to a funeral caused some resentment.

Eling has had a church since Saxon days. In 1654 Oliver Cromwell's son Richard (see Hursley) solemnised the marriage of Thomas Burgess and Elizabeth Russsell—both staunch Puritans, no doubt. In the churchyard is an epitaph dated 1703 to William Mansbridge of Cadnam:

> Stop Reader, pray, and read my fate,
> What caused my life to terminate:
> For theivs by night when in my bed
> Broak up my hous and shot me dead.

John Stigant's shipyard at Eling built the 16-gun man-o'-war *Wrenn* in 1695; John Warwick junior built the *Goldfinch* (10 guns) in 1808, and the *Spy* (16 guns) in 1913. Merchantmen berthed below the mill until well into the days of steam. Now, with the popularity of yachting, the sails are back.

Eling Great Marsh, on the tongue of reclaimed land between Eling Creek and the Redbridge Channel (the mouth of the Test) was enclosed in 1941. Although four years later it was recorded that "some of the inhabitants enjoy a grazing right" on the Furlongs, an attempt by the parish council to register both the Marsh and the Furlongs was abandoned.

A plan to extend Southampton Docks by reclaiming more land at the head of the estuary would have prevented public access to the water on the last remaining stretch of foreshore, at Goatey Beach, but the danger seems to have been averted. Meanwhile it is worth noting that this enclave of fields dominated by pylons and hemmed in by industry is the prospect which inspired Isaac Watts, standing on the opposite shore at Millbrook, to write: "There is a land of pure delight."

Eling has lost its shipyards and gained a timber-yard, lost its soap-boiling works and gained a tar distillery. It lost its fair, once a two-day affair with a pony and cattle market on the first day and a pleasure fair on the second, in 1905. It had become so rowdy that several unsuccessful attempts to ban it were made before the Secretary of State finally agreed to its abolition "for the convenience and advantage of the public". In 1951 it was, in a more genteel form, revived.

Various claims have been made that Totton and/or Eling is the largest village or parish in the country. A former council chairman put the whole thing in perspective when he defined it as the largest parish administered by a parish council. He has also put on record that its population, which included the inhabitants of Calmore, Rumbridge, Testwood, and Totton, was in 1939 22,222. This was the number of people the council had to supply with gas-masks as Britain awaited the outbreak of the Second World War!

# Ellingham 🦚

In Ellingham church is the tomb of Dame Alicia Lisle of Moyles Court, the 70-year-old widow of a supporter of Cromwell. In July 1685 she gave shelter to two fugitives from the Battle of Sedgemoor during the unsuccessful rebellion led by the Duke of Monmouth. They were a nonconformist minister, John Hicks, and a Somerset lawyer, Richard Nelthorp. Dame Alicia, whose husband had been proscribed by Charles II's government and assassinated in Switzerland, was arrested after the discovery of the fugitives and taken to Winchester.

The jury thought the evidence against her was insufficient but the notorious Judge Jeffreys, who had told one witness he was a "prevaricating, shuffling, snivelling, lying rascal", bullied the jurymen until they brought in a verdict of guilty, whereupon he ordered her to be dragged on a hurdle to the place of execution and burned alive. After public protests James II altered the sentence to beheading—and four years later Parliament, petitioned by her two daughters, annulled the conviction on the grounds of Jeffreys' unlawful conduct of the case.

Moyles Court, where a court baron was held in medieval times, took its name from a family called Meole who held it in the 14th century. In this century it belonged to the Earl of Normanton, but became a school after he sold it in 1962.

The Domesday Book records that "Adelingham" was held by Cola—perhaps the huntsman who also held Langley—and until this century a family named Cole had a farm near the church. And the church where we began, is where we end: a memorial commemorates not only the three men from Ellingham who were killed in the First World War, but the 52 who returned "neither blind nor maimed".

# Eversley 🦚

Charles Kingsley wrote *The Water Babies* at Eversley Rectory, though his inspiration is less likely to have been the Blackwater stream than the River Itchen, which he knew from fishing holidays (see Itchen Abbas). He came to Eversley as a 23-year-old curate in 1842 and immediately found himself in charge, as the rector disappeared on a six-week holiday abroad.

Living in lodgings at a cottage called The Brewery—now Dial House—he soon explored the village with its green occupied by cricketers at weekends and hens during the week, and its "scattered red brick cottages each with its large neat garden and clipt yews and hollies"—though he later commented that five-sixth of the parish consisted of fir, forest and moorland.

He came to know and admire the villagers—broomsquires and peat-cutters as well as farm labourers—claiming somewhat fancifully that a "dash of wild forest blood from gypsy and highwayman" made them shrewder than men of purer Saxon stock. His typical—or perhaps ideal— parishioner was "dark-haired, ruddy and tall of bone, swaggering in his youth, but when he grows old a thorough gentleman—reserved, stately and courteous as a prince".

He relieved the rector of teaching, despite the "heat and the smell" generated in a schoolroom only ten feet square. Susan Chitty records in her biography, *The Beast And The Monk*, how when the rector finally fled to avoid a scandal Kingsley pulled the neglected parish together—visiting people in their homes, helping with the threshing, mowing and haymaking, talking to farmworkers about hedging and ditching, and to farmers about the rotation of crops. Lady Chitty discovered that some of his parishioners found him positively nosey, and she talked to a man who admitted that his grandfather had thrown stones at Kingsley's carriage.

It was his manner, rather than his intentions, which must have irritated. Visiting a sick man in a ground-floor bedroom he rushed upstairs with an augur and bored ventilation holes in the ceiling above the bed. The cottage must have smelled worse than the schoolroom.

Eversley is near enough to Windsor forest to have contributed its quota of deer-poachers. Kingsley's reluctance to condemn them continued a parish tradition, for an earlier church had provided sanctuary for poachers and other refugees from the law.

In the 18th century it was believed that a dip in the sea prevented anyone bitten by a rabid dog from going mad. On October 2nd, 1770, the parish spent £2 19s 6d on sending

Daniel Traish to Southampton for this purpose. The last man to be offered this salt-water treatment, one Mayers, said he'd rather go mad, thank you: instead he emigrated to Australia, and made a fortune. It turned out that the dog hadn't had rabies in any case.

# Faccombe 🦢

Students of the vernacular may surmise why the name of Faccombe Upstreet has fallen into disuse. It was so named to distinguish it from the settlement at the lower end of the village, Faccombe Netherton, where the manor which crumbled in 1379 was reputed to be the seventh building on the site.

The village first took its name from a Saxon chieftain, Facca. The "combe" bit, meaning valley, is of course from a language older than his—Welsh, or Ancient British, surviving in (for instance) Cwm Rhondda. The next village, a cleft in the chalk downs called simply Combe, is by some freak of frontiers in Berkshire.

There was a 13th-century church dedicated to St Michael at Netherton, but some 600 years later the centre of population (the term is relative) had shifted uphill, and the church of St Barnabas was built to serve the village now known more simply as Faccombe.

# Farringdon 🦢

"A most appalling horror of scarlet brick and tile . . . a suburban palace of varieties." So much for the do-it-almost-yourself efforts of a former rector, the Reverend T. H. Massey, who, with the help of a single labourer, built a private school at Farringdon with which he supplemented his stipend. "Massey's Folly" became a church school and a parish hall in 1925, but had not mellowed in time for the harsh verdict of the author of *Highways and Byways in Hampshire*. Mr Massey and his predecessor between them served the parish for 122 years. A curate at one time was Gilbert White (see Selborne),

72

who used to preach in summer from the steps of a stone cross in the churchyard.

A tradition which had died out by the turn of the century was a variation on the theme of virgins' crowns (see Abbott's Ann). Garlands of white flowers were hung on pillars in the church at the funeral of each "virtuous unmarried girl" from the parish.

Persons who were not virtuous tended to be subjected to the procedure known as skimmington, defined in the Shorter Oxford Dictionary as a "ludicrous procession, formerly common in villages and country districts, usually intended to bring ridicule or odium upon a woman or her husband where the one was unfaithful to, or illtreated, the other (1634)". The practice of skimmington was not uncommon, but it appears to have been embraced by the villagers of Farringdon with particular fervour. Whether this was through the lack of a marriage guidance counsellor or because they simply loved making a racket we shall never know. We do know that in the village the "rough music", produced by banging on pots and pans or anything else that would make a noise, would be kept up at intervals for a week.

# Fawley

The Royal Family has an interest in Fawley which it may not realise. Her Majesty's ancestors have been traced back to the Saxon kings of Wessex, and it was somewhere near Calshot that Cerdic, founder of the dynasty, established his beach-head some 1500 years ago.

Industry established its own beach-head in 1920 when Anglo-American Oil put up a modest installation on the Cadland Estate. Esso Petroleum swallowed Anglo-American and in 1951 opened their giant refinery in parkland laid out by Capability Brown, and tore down Cadland House: though by then, like Manderley in the opening paragraphs of Daphne du Maurier's *Rebecca*, it was an elegant fire-damaged shell.

There had been industry of a sort before the refinery— saltpans along the shoreline, notably in the neighbourhood of Ashlett Creek, where there was also a mill. Something akin to forced labour went on in the poorhouse, a building behind the church later divided into three cottages. In 1797 the inmates' earnings totalled £13 4s 9d—payment for knitting and flax-spinning by the girls and women, and hemp-picking and casual labour by men and boys.

Earlier, men had intermittently been paid a few shillings for keeping watch on Southampton Water. In 1667, at the time of the Dutch raids on the South Coast, John Wilson was hired to keep watch "when the Flemans [Flemings] were within the Isle of Wight".

Parish registers also show that in 1694 Philip Rossiter died at the age of 105, and in the following year John Yetman died at the same age "as he himself reported". Yet I've read some-where that the "miasma" arising from the marshes was so noxious at least to a series of short-lived incumbents that the parish was known for a while as "Fawley Kill-Parson".

In 1830 at the time of the Labourers' Revolt 300 men "armed with staves" arrived at Eaglehurst, a big house facing the Isle of Wight, and demanded of Lord Cavan that their wages be raised to 2s a day—and that the workhouse-master be dismissed. But His Lordship arrested the ringleader and the men dispersed. A less truculent visitor the following year was Queen Victoria. Perhaps she was given a room with a view towards the island because later, thinking of buying Eaglehurst as a royal retreat, she decided on Osborne instead.

In Victorian days Fawley was a compact little village with most of its needs in the way of trade catered for by the Bowman family. Mr Frederick Bowman, who died in 1958, was one of the first people in the district to drive a car.

The railway came in 1925: it linked the infant refinery with the Southampton–Weymouth line ten miles away at Totton. The last track to be constructed under the Light Railways Act of 1896, it did not require Parliamentary sanction but only a Board of Trade Order. The consequent relaxation of the nor-mal regulations on manned level-crossings is still a matter of controversy now that the only trains are strings of tank wag-gons from the refinery.

Workers on the vast petro-chemical complex which has now engulfed the west side of Southampton Water were in 1958 provided with platforms at that most happily named of stations, Hardley Halt. But the line was closed to passengers in 1966, and efforts by the Trades Council to persuade British Rail to re-open it were dismissed in 1975 as "not feasible".

Before the expansion of the refinery the track made a useful but illegal route from Hythe to Cadland Creek, in crossing which it marooned the boathouse belonging to Cadland House. So another, reached by a narrow embankment among the reeds, was built in the marshes on the seaward side of the line.

Overhead, at one time, cruised the flying-boats which BOAC ran from Southampton Docks for a brief period after the war on the former South African route of the old Imperial Airways system. Those flying, or rather non-flying, white elephants known as Princesses, designed to revitalise this mode of transport, lay for years cocooned off the RAF base at Calshot Spit—now used by the county council as an "activities centre". It was to the RAF camp that the islanders from Tristan da Cunha were brought after the volcanic eruption of 1962, and a model of one of their longboats was placed in the church to commemorate their stay.

The official guide points out that 40 per cent of the land in the parish is still farmed. The area between Fawley old village and Blackfield, now marked on maps as The Pentagon, used to be called Barebones because "you could grow neither stick nor stem on that land". The first house to be built there, on a corner which now backs on to an extensive housing estate, was "The Treshams". It was, and is, the home of Eric Jones-Evans, admired and respected then as the village doctor and now (he retired the day the National Health Service came in) as the last living link with Irving, Tree, and other giants of the Victorian theatre whose traditions he has maintained as an actor, a playwright, a theatrical historian, and a larger-than-life personality.

# Grateley 🌿

The Roman Portway, with parts overgrown and others still in use as metalled roads or grass tracks, used to connect Sarum with Silchester. The section that ran through Grateley was still in use, 17 centuries after it was laid down, as part of the main highway between London and Exeter. Perhaps Grateley's good communications provided the reason for its choice by King Athelstan in Saxon times as a site for his parliament. Though both roads to Exeter now run south of it, the village must be a rare one in being still served by a main line railway station.

The 12th-century church has fragments of glass dating from not much later which were removed from Salisbury Cathedral in the 17th century—about the time when Dame Johanna Elton left a guinea to the parish clerk so long as her grave was kept tidy and provided with flowers.

Rationing in the Second World War meant that cash only could be distributed to the needy rather than "good ox beef" at Christmas and cheese at Easter, as directed by the Lord of the Manor in 1787. He left £300 on which the interest was to be used for this bi-annual charity. If funds permitted, potatoes and peas were to be dished out at Easter as well. The sale of a piece of land in 1943 meant that its rent was no longer available to provide deserving villagers with coats and waistcoats, as directed by the terms of another charity dating back to 1707. Originally it had been stipulated that the garments should be green.

# Grayshott ❧

Most books about Hampshire ignore Grayshott, and indeed unless you can find Boundary Road it is difficult to be sure where Hindhead and Surrey end, and where Grayshott and Hampshire begin. Margaret Lane, who knows more about Flora Thompson than anyone else, wrote in 1957 that the author of *Lark Rise to Candleford* went at the age of 20 to work at the post-office in "the little Surrey village of Grayshott". That was in 1897: Flora lived first with the postmaster's family and then in lodgings. This was a prudent move, since he quarrelled violently with his wife and eventually—after Flora had left the district—murdered her with a carving knife.

Residents of this border country at the turn of the century

76

included Bernard Shaw and Conan Doyle: Flora, "unregarded as a piece of furniture" on her side of the counter, used to listen to their conversation. "Perhaps these 'great examples' encouraged my desire to express myself in writing", she noted later, "but I cannot remember the time when I did not wish and mean to write". In *Heatherley*, the fictionalised account of her three years at Grayshott, she relates how Laura—her other self—"several times heard Mr Bernard Shaw lecture on Socialism. He was freely interrupted and questioned by his audience, to which at that time the initials G.B.S. had no special significance".

Flora Thompson recounts how Heatherley-Grayshott began to prosper for a while. "The villagers dressed better, had more amusements, wider ideas, and a better time generally. Some building was done and many looked forward to seeing in their own lifetime their village develop into a kind of garden city." Instead Hindhead, which she calls "the other settlement", being in "the choicest part of the hilly scenery which had always been the chief attraction to visitors", was to be the area of development. When Flora returned to the district 20 years later she found that building plots at Heatherley which had optimistically been staked out had "reverted to heath".

Had development gone ahead it might have meant the end in Grayshott of a rural craft which still survives here and there in the north of the county. In *Craftsmen at Work* John Norwood devotes a chapter to a local broomsquire, Mr Peter Burrows, whom he found carrying on his family tradition of making brooms on the customary "horse", or bench, with birch twigs and—preferably—chestnut handles.

# Greywell ✺

Local people used to spell and pronounce it Grewell, says Robert Potter in *Hampshire Harvest*—adding that Grewell Silks were famous in Tudor times. Greywell Mill on the Whitewater, mentioned in the Domesday Book, survived in successive forms until 1930 when the great elm water-wheel finally "gave up the ghost". It had a longer life than Greywell Tunnel, dug in 1793 through Gruel Hill to save the Basingstoke Canal a six-mile loop and to meet Lord Tylney's objections that his estate would be practically encircled.

The tunnel had no towpath and bargees had to "leg it" against the brick sides or roof. One of the longest in the south of England, it was nearly a mile in length and ran 140 feet below the surface. It collapsed in 1872 just after a bargee from Mapledurwell, called Burrows, had got through. In October 1827 a lad by the name of Jordan had drowned in the tunnel and there were several other drownings in the open canal which was also used for ducking people suspected of various offences, from picking pockets to "unnatural crime".

P. A. L. Vine's *London's Lost Route to Basingstoke* looks in detail at the story of this 37-mile dead end canal, originally intended to connect London and Guildford with Southampton via Andover or Winchester, and Bristol via Newbury. The original company planted firs on its land at Greywell and elsewhere as part of what it hoped would be a profitable sideline. However, profit was never the canal's strong point and after various vicissitudes the Basingstoke end has now been filled in, and the stretch from Greywell to its junction with the Wey Navigation near Godalming is operated jointly as a leisure project by Hampshire and Surrey County Councils. But in the beginning Greywell had a wharf of its own with a timber yard on the north bank, and a sawpit and coal store opposite.

In the 17th century there were hop gardens around the village: hence the name of a stream, Hopeyard Piddle. Another was named after the malthouse, too.

This century's Greywell is happy to be away from any traffic artery, waterborne or otherwise. In 1971 it was voted Hampshire's best-kept village.

# Hamble

The rising ground on the angle of the River Hamble and Southampton Water provided a site and a name for Hamble le Rice, otherwise Hamble Rise. The river was a useful waterway for traders and invaders (see Botley and Bursledon) and the high ground was an obvious defensive position. There was a shore battery on Hamble Common in the middle of the 19th century; in 1881, the First Hampshire Volunteer Artillery Corps were using an ancient 20-pounder to supplement their 40-pounder Armstrongs when the veteran gun exploded. Sergeant Burt, whose leg was broken, became the first Volunteer ever to be awarded a pension.

Hamble's defences must have been rudimentary or non-existent when the village was raided by the French in 1377. The French returned some 400 years later—as prisoners from the Napoleonic Wars. Of the thousands who were interned in Hampshire (see Bishop's Waltham and Odiham) many caught their first glimpse of England when brought ashore at Hamble and placed under guard in the great barn near Hamble Church prior to dispersal. It is recorded in the parish register that in 1795 Betty Emm—the surname is still not uncommon in Hampshire and Wiltshire—married "Coranne La Goffe, one of the soldiers now at Hamble".

William of Wykeham bought Hamble Manor as an endowment for Winchester College in 1391, and another connection with Winchester was the annual "tribute" of oysters paid to St Swithun's Priory. The oyster beds flourished as late as 1850 but Hamble was an active fishing port on a modest scale until 1914 or thereabouts. Trawlers would bring back North Sea scallops, and lobsters and shellfish from West Country and Irish waters. Odd knife-marks on the church door are explained by the tradition of a fisherman making a downward cut before setting sail and adding a horizontal cut when he reached harbour again, to make a thanksgiving cross for a calm sea and a prosperous voyage—or at least a safe return.

By 1919 the functional was beginning to be superseded by the picturesque and a visitor described Hamble as "the quaintest of tiny seaports". Working fishermen and visitors of 50 years ago would have been more than startled by a foreglimpse of today's rows of pleasure-craft, packed together like dates in a box. Also by the behaviour and appearance ashore and afloat not of the serious sailor but of the female of the visiting species; summer migrants with improbable plumage and shrill cries reputed to shatter crystal at fifty paces.

Moored at Hamble until 1968 was the wooden-hulled HMS *President*, better known as the Training Ship *Mercury*. The original ship and shore establishment were provided by Charles Arthur Hoare and were run after his death by the England cricketer C. B. Fry and his wife. Arthur Mee wrote that "the basis of training is religious, and every gift for beauty that a boy may possess, such as a love of poetry or an aptitude for drawing, is encouraged directly it is perceived". I'm bound to add that a friend of mine who was sent there after his parents' death finds the description—and there's a lot more in the same vein—totally unrecognisable. So did a contemporary at *Mercury* of my friend; he happened to review—most generously—this book in 1980. He commented how some boys in the ship "saw Fry only twice—once when he made them run in bare feet on gravel, and once when he lined them up and practised casting between their heads".

Twentieth-century developments at Hamble, the yacht marina apart, have included an oil company's depot, aircraft manufacture, and an airfield at which particular attention has been paid for many years to the training of pilots for night flying—much to the distress of a good many local residents.

# Hambledon

R.C.G.

The Bat and Ball
Broadhalfpenny Down, Hambledon-

80

To those bits of the world which used to be red on the map Hambledon means cricket, so let's start by recording—or rather re-recording—that in 1777 the village played All England for one thousand guineas, winning by an innings and 68 runs. Hambledon was the nursery rather than the birthplace of the game, and after their famous victory it was 20 years before the cricketers of Hambledon yielded their position to their rivals at Marylebone.

The much older cricket ground at Broad Ha'penny Down was bought by Winchester College in 1926, and it was from a bat and ball preserved at the college that replicas were copied for a "Regency" match played at Hambledon in 1946. Enthusiasm for the Prince Regent in his own day accounted perhaps for the fact that for a time the famous Bat and Ball Inn up on the down—kept by the cricketing Nyrens—was known as the George Hotel.

Other royal connections include the assent by James I in 1612 to the holding of fairs in February and September as well as the weekly market—letters patent for the holding of the fair being stamped with the words Broad Half Penny. The traditions of building a "bower" for feasting and dancing on special occasions continued through Queen Victoria's diamond jubilee and the coronation of George V.

In the 18th century Henry Hammond had a smithy at the corner of the High Street and Cam's Lane. The business was continued by his son Harry, and passed to his nephew, George Lott, thus giving rise to the name Lott's Corner. There has been a continuity of family if not of profession. George's son Harry took over on his father's retirement in 1906. The smithy closed in 1934, though Hambledon is one of the few villages where cars still look out of place. Harry died in 1954 but his daughter continued to live at Forge Cottage and, with her husband, managed the shop next door.

Terry Norman's excellent photographic history of Hambledon and Denmead reproduces this 18th-century acrostic advertisement for an earlier shopkeeper at Hambledon:

# GOOD NEWS!

A native who lives in this sweet little village,
Judging from what I have seen,

Will sell groceries cheap, and with others compete, in
Hambledon and elsewhere, as far as you've been.
I say give him a trial, it will be worth your while
To purchase all articles sold at this shop;
To housekeepers all, I say give him a call;
Encourage A.J.W., for his goods are tip-top.
Now I wish for to call your special attention—
Home-baked Bread from flour that's ne'er crossed the seas.
A regular judge had pronounced it as good,
Mind, do not forget, he sells the best Coals and Wood.

Green Teas and Black Teas, whose flavours are fine,
Raisins and Currants in quality prime,
Oatmeal and Tapioca, recommended by Gooding,
Candied Lemon-peel and Nutmeg for cakes and puddings;
Each article sold shall be really most prime,
Recommend you he can, all he sells in his line;

Hambledon is a place that supplies Home-Cured Bacon,
As I've tasted the same I can't be mistaken;
Mixed Pickles and Sauces that will make you eat hearty.
Biscuits of all kinds, to supply your tea-party,
Lobsters potted, as well as good Salmon;
Eighty yards from this shop is a brewery, by Gammon;
Don't forget that Whittenham keeps a Donkey and Cart,
Outstripping all others, for speed he is smart.
Now I'll finish off here, or I'll get in a mess; so
            remember the CAPITALS bear the address.

82

Daniel Lunn of Hambledon, brewer of pale ale, sold out to Crowley of Alton (later engulfed by Watney), but local production continued and the family connection was kept up for some time. One of the more distinguished of English wines is produced at the vineyard which Sir Guy Salisbury-Jones established at Hambledon in 1953.

Much earlier, there came into production a rare apple known locally as the Hambledon Dozen: this is nothing to do with the Twelfth Man at cricket but a corruption of Deux-Ans. The apple, as I am happy to confirm with the help of a friend who has a specimen in his garden at Chilbolton, keeps for two years.

# Hartley Mauditt

Yes, well, you won't find the village now: but there are still traces. All that's left above ground is the church and a farm and a cottage or two, so some writers have been tempted to believe that the name is a variation on *maudit*, the French for accursed. However, a family named Mauditt held the manor when the Domesday Book was compiled. By the 18th century it belonged to the Stowells, and Lady Stowell far preferred living in the village to staying at their town residence. To spite her, Lord Stowell, who did not share her preference for rural peace, pulled it down: which, as they say, left Her Ladyship no alternative.

It also left the village no nucleus. Things fell apart. Only an aerial view now indicates the alignment of long-vanished cottages between the church and the one cottage that still remains. Perhaps the dwellings that disappeared once housed Zachary Mansell (weaver) and William Mitchell (tailor) who in 1588 planned a protest against the cost of living. Corn was unduly dear because farmers had taken to planting a more profitable crop used by cloth-makers to dye their products—woad. Their idea, never put into operation, was to fire the beacon erected to provide early warning of the approach of the Spanish Armada—a sort of Elizabethan Fylingdales, only less of a blot on the landscape—arm the villagers who would then (they hoped) assemble, and persuade them to take over the granaries.

When I first looked into the 12th-century church in 1945 or thereabouts there was that smell of damp hassocks and mice which indicates ecclesiastical neglect, or at least disuse; even its dedication had been forgotten. But in 1959 a woman who spent her childhood in the parish described—in the *Southern Evening Echo*—the arrival, when she was a girl, of a new rector, the Reverend Arthur Kay Boustead.

He put in land-drains, had the fences repaired to stop cattle trampling all over the graves, and "had a little tower built". A frail, gentle man with an asthmatic wife, he arrived with five children who soon totalled six. Often he played the organ as well as conducting the service. His eyesight deteriorated and before going to hospital for an operation he got his son to take him round the parish "just in case"—but the treatment was successful.

The same correspondent recalled playing hide-and-seek in the remains of the manor house before the cellar entrances were trodden down by cattle, and remembered the days of wide hopfields and busy kilns. The school was closed in 1936, its numbers having dwindled to eight children from scattered houses and cottages. In 1959 what remained was officially classified as an ancient monument.

# Hartley Wintney

Voted Hampshire's best-kept village in 1973, Hartley Wintney is a series of greens and commons edged by groups of houses. The original nucleus was the priory on Winta's island. "Eye" or "eyot" is an old word for island, which in this case was not an island at all but a tongue of land between two branches of the river Hart. Winta was probably a Saxon and the later name "Winchester Island" was a misapprehension based on the fact that eventually the priory came under the jurisdiction of the Bishop of Winchester.

84

David Gorsky writes in *The Old Village of Hartley Wintney* that the five events by which it was most affected were the expulsion of the nuns in 1536; the construction of the turnpike road in 1767 and the London and Southampton railway in 1838; the erection of St John's Church in 1870; and the coming of the motorway a century later. This last cut off the priory from the settlement to which it gave its name.

Elvetham Park was enclosed as early as 1403 and the peasants turned out of their common fields. In 1536 it was the turn of the nuns to be evicted when Henry VIII gave their priory to his cellarer; four days earlier he had married Jane Seymour, whose family held Elvetham.

The turnpike road—later to become the A30—and its London–Exeter traffic brought about a gentle 18th-century equivalent of ribbon development at Hartley Row with shops and houses between the Lamb and the Phoenix. The coach trade dwindled with the coming of the railway, but a tanhouse and a brewery—the former now the site of a factory, the latter burned down this century—added to the basic local industries of farming and brick-making. Parochial rather than private enterprise resulted in an early water supply for the village, and a gasworks. The latter made it possible to light a mile of the London Road—which, with its straight stretch through Hartford Bridge Flats, was a temptation to early motorists.

L. T. C. Rolt—engineer, car, railway, and canal enthusiast and writer—recorded in his autobiography *Landscape with Machines* how in 1934 his friend John Passini introduced him to "a marvellous pub he had discovered at Hartley Wintney". This was the Phoenix: then kept by Tim Carson, a devotee like themselves of motor racing. In his yard was a coachbuilder's premises used as a filling station. Rolt and Passini converted it into the Phoenix Green Garage, unofficial headquarters of the Vintage Sports Car Club and birthplace of Rolt's "Phoenix Special"—the rear half of a 1922 GN Popular and the front half of a Bugatti. Destined for Brooklands, it was left locked up in the garage when the garage was commandeered on the outbreak of war and disappeared without trace.

Rolt describes the commonsense attitude of the local constable ("Evildoers were his concern but the sharp eye he kept cocked for the malefactor would become afflicted with blindness when confronted by the technical offender") and records the difficulty of getting his customers to pay their bills ("the local farmers, I am sorry to say, were the worst payers").

It is a miracle that Hartley Wintney has managed to survive almost unscathed being sliced across from end to end by a series of busy lines of communications. Its open spaces must have acted as lungs: and perhaps, paradoxically enough, the motorway turned out to be a lifeline which came just in time.

# Hayling ✑

Divided by a natural waist into North and South Hayling, the island is connected to the Hampshire mainland by a bridge over what used to be the wadeway. Rivalry between north and south, confined this century to little more than a ritual tug-of-war, broke out occasionally in the past but islanders would unite over such local problems as maintaining a ferry service over the wadeway and on national and international matters.

In 1694 the North took the lead, with 30 villagers subscribing three guineas apiece to assist in the prosecution of "a vigorous war against France". The subscription list was put up on the wall of St Peter's Church—originally erected, incidentally, by Norman conquerors. Perhaps the sailor whose ghost occupies a rear pew from time to time died fighting the French: he wears a tarred pigtail and a straw hat.

Of course, it was seaborne invasions which tended to preoccupy the island. The defence was not as comprehensively equipped as it might have been: in medieval times the parish armoury included "1 corselet, 7 harquebuses, 17 bows unfurnished and 12 bows furnished". Anti-invasion equipment at the time of the Spanish Armada was in a sorry state, "many of the men being rawly furnished, some lacketh of a Headpiece, some a sord, some one thing and some another". In 1940, before their transformation into the Home Guard, the Local Defence Volunteers had 19 shotguns, a few revolvers (where from?)—and of course armbands.

Another enemy against whom Hayling Islanders readily closed ranks was the Revenue Man. One smuggler, William Clark of Woodgaston Cottage, equipped his fishing-boat with a false bottom for contraband but somehow it was discovered. Clark laid about the customs official with a cutlass by way of resisting arrest but was overpowered, sentenced, and imprisoned—dying before his three-year term was up.

The wadeway, which in its natural state could be jumped at low tide by a man on horseback, was dredged in the 1820s as part of a scheme to connect Portsmouth Harbour with the Thames by way of the Wey and Arun Canal. This prompted the building in 1824 of a tollbridge; and, despite the fact that exemption from tolls was granted only to members of the Royal Family, servicemen in uniform, postmen on duty, voters going to the polls, and worshippers going to church, the development of Hayling promptly began. Incidentally the total raised by tolls until a new bridge was built 136 years later in 1960 was £28,500.

The results of the introduction of the tollbridge were discernible within a decade. A guide of 1836 pronounced that: "Capitalist enterprise has converted a barren beach into a little paradise". The process was, for good or bad, accelerated by the arrival of the railway in 1867—though less quickly than elsewhere. It was day-trippers rather than islanders or long-term holidaymakers who came by rail which crossed the wadeway by a swingbridge. Edwin Course relates in the Secondary and Branch Lines volume of his history of *The Railways of Southern England* how it was operated: "As navigational rights still existed round the island, the bridge had an opening span and alongside it was a signal box. This was equipped with home and distant signals, suitably interlocked, so that they could only be pulled off when the span was set for the railway. Needless to say, the opening of the bridge was quite a performance, necessitating the services of both a signalman and a lengthman. The signalman uncoupled the signal wires which crossed the span, while the lengthman unbolted the fishplates. The master of a vessel had to watch for three signs, which were hoisted on the flagstaff which adjoined the opening span. First, a white flag by day or a white light by night acknowledged that the vessel had been seen; if no train was due a black ball by day or a green light by night was hoisted and, finally, when the span was opened this was indicated by a red flag by day and a red lamp by night."

Weight restrictions on the bridge meant that the only locomotives used were diminutive tank engines—Terriers of London Brighton and South Coast origin, of which one was eventually turned into a unique pub sign outside the Hayling Billy. And it was the cost of replacing the bridge—£400,000—which was the deciding factor in closing down the entire branch in 1963.

F. G. S. Thomas records in *The King Holds Hayling* how an 18th-century vicar, the Reverend Isaac Skelton, told an official church inquiry that he performed his duties at Hayling but lived in Havant for the sake of his health. This must appear something of a turn-up for the holy book in the eyes of the tens of thousands of holidaymakers who have swarmed over the island during the present century.

# Hedge End

What sort of people used to live at Hedge End before the housing estates spread over the sloping fields? One summary was "gypsies, farm labourers and strawberry growers". Whoever they were, they didn't take kindly to authority, and took particular exception to the toll road (see Bursledon) going to Bitterne and Southampton.

In 1929 the Mayor of that city, Councillor Maurice Pugh, visited Hedge End to discuss what by then was officially recognised as a "bar to progress and development", the tollgates. Villagers had reached the same conclusion some time previously, and when the official party turned up it was found that somebody had anticipated them by removing the gates the night before. Tollkeepers must have had to be a pretty forceful lot, though by all accounts one of the most effective of them was Granny Allen, whose height was only 4 feet 6 inches or thereabouts. But the freeing of the gates is still remembered in Hedge End: the 50th anniversary of liberation day was commemorated by the purchase of a public seat—and one of the contributors was Councillor Pugh's son Ronald.

Hedge End in its early days was called "Botley's poor relation" and indeed it used to be thought that it had no name but "Botley Common" until late Victorian times—but it is probable that the name Hedge End came into use some 250 years ago.

# Highclere

"Plenty of water and masses of rhododendrons." It sounds an informal description of Highclere Park but was written a century ago when the words had more precise meanings. It owes its design, including the lake, to Henry Herbert, first Earl of Carnarvon. The castle was once the principal country residence of the Bishops of Winchester and in the 14th century the original manor was the administrative headquarters—complete with outbuildings including a brewery—of an extensive episcopal domain which stretched south to Burghclere and eastwards beyond Ecchinswell. The house was rebuilt by the third Earl between 1839–42 in a Renaissance style. His architect was Sir Charles Barry, the man responsible for the Houses of Parliament; but most people will have been unable to see much more than a pinnacle or two by which to make a comparison since the park, compared to other great estates, maintains an air of aloofness. This is certainly not true of its owner. The present Lord Carnarvon is a man of considerable bounce and charm. He is currently basking in the reputation of a successful author, with two very amusing autobiographical books to his credit. His father, the fifth Earl (he who discovered the tomb of Tutankhamun) is buried at the top of nearby Beacon Hill.

The cone of a Cedar of Lebanon in the park was brought back by a former rector, the Reverend Isaac Miles. He was a scholarly traveller and his daughter was later described by Mrs Elizabeth Montagu, who lived nearby, as "an ancient gentlewoman skilled in Latin, dipped in Greek and absorbed in Hebrew. . . . By this learned person was young Mr Pococke skilled in antique lore. His gingerbread was marked with Greek characters and his bread and butter . . . . in Arabic. He had a mummy for his doll and a little pyramid for his playhouse." Whether or not it was the result of this early cramming, Richard Pococke later became reasonably well known in 18th-century ecclesiastical circles, becoming Bishop of Meath:

and he travelled even more extensively than his grandfather, Mr Miles.

A later parson, Canon Portal, is credited with having founded the first thrift club in the county. It met for a church service on Whit Mondays and members then marched in procession to the park—the girls in white with hats wreathed in flowers. There was lunch at the Carnarvon Arms and then it was back to the park for an afternoon of festivities, with further sustenance for those who required it in the form of specially-baked gingerbread.

At one time there was a flourishing blanket mill in the village, so the law to protect the industry enacted in 1668 was no doubt enforced with more enthusiasm than in other districts. Until 1817, by which time observance was obviously less strict, nothing but wool was allowed for "shrouds, shirts, and shifts" at interments.

It is tempting to imagine that those who transgressed this law were menaced by the monster reputed to live in a yew tree at the entrance to the church, but he must have been in occupation some centuries earlier. Described in some records as a grampus, he—or possibly she—was exorcised by bell, book and candle and banished to the Red Sea for a thousand years.

Certainly I couldn't find any trace of him: perhaps *any* sea would provide a more suitable habitat than a yew tree for a creature that is defined as a "blowing, spouting, blunt-headed delphinoid cetacean".

# Hinton Ampner

The "Ampner" reveals the village's connection with the Priory of St Swithun at Winchester and its almoner; and its history is largely that of its manor—which has been told with scholarly affection by Ralph Dutton, historian and former High Sheriff of Hampshire, whose home it is. In 1960 a fire broke out in his library and, hampered by a shortage of water, firemen were unable to save the building: but their efforts were recognised when he invited 130 of them to a party after the manor had been rebuilt.

Another Hinton Ampner House, with 21 bedrooms and outbuildings including a brewhouse, was burned down in Tudor times. Various buildings have stood on the site. One was let in the 1760s to a Mr and Mrs Ricketts, whose experience of what we should today call poltergeist phenomena was alarming indeed. Doors opened and shut of their own accord, groans and flutterings were heard, and "human voices joined the general cacophony". Mrs Ricketts' brother, Admiral Jarvis—later Earl St Vincent—and a friend stayed up one night in separate rooms. Hearing noises, they rushed out with pistols cocked, but nobody was there. The admiral suggested the Ricketts family should, so to speak, abandon ship, and the house remained empty for some years.

When in 1793, the owner, Lord Stawell, had it pulled down, a skull was discovered. Villagers considered this proof of their suspicions that a previous occupant and his sister-in-law had—hence the hauntings—murdered their bastard child.

# Holybourne 🦢

Still not quite overwhelmed by its proximity to Alton, Holybourne retains despite new housing estates something of the village charm which must have endeared it to the Victorian novelist Mrs Gaskell. Her husband was a Unitarian minister in Manchester and much of her writing contrasted—to use one of her own titles—North and South. Her books were notable for social conscience without pious sighing. She bought "The Lawns" on the main street with the proceeds of her writing and planned to give it to her husband as a sort of retirement present, to mark the completion of her novel Sons and Daughters, but died suddenly at her new house before the last instalments were written.

Roman coins and other more substantial remains have been found in the parish. Cuckoo's Corner, on the east of the village, is believed by some authorities to have been the point where the Roman road from Chichester to Silchester crossed the Pilgrims' Way to Canterbury.

# Hordle 🦡

People who remember the village before the First World War tend to say that it isn't what it was. Anyone with a memory spanning 500 years would probably add that it isn't *where* it was, either. Erosion, a serious problem today, has over the centuries eaten back the coastline and with it (the extent of its appetite varies from account to account) an earlier settlement and the saltpans, reputed to have been a flourishing local industry from at least the 11th century to the 19th. Also a church—the bells of which, imaginative persons insist, may on occasion be heard ringing beneath the waves.

Extensive dredging operations carried out a hundred years ago produced, however, no archaeological evidence of the drowned village, with or without church, or if they did it went unrecognised. What the dredgers were after were ironstone nodules deposited on the seabed: they were used at one time in the manufacture of a sort of submarine cement.

In the churchyard—the present churchyard, that is—lie the bodies of Mary Ann Girling and 11 of her followers, leader and members of a short-lived religious sect known as the New Forest Shakers. They never lived in the forest itself but occupied New Forest Lodge in Vaggs Lane, later renamed Hordle Grange and used as a nursing home.

Mrs Girling, believed by her followers to be a reincarnation of Christ, hailed from East Anglia and later moved to London, but in 1872 a wealthy supporter found the community its new headquarters at Hordle. In three years their numbers had swelled to 150 or so—a third of them children, with women outnumbering men by roughly two to one. Probably it was this which aroused suspicions of immorality, though the rule of celibacy was so strict that the sexes even ate separately. Mother Girling's Shakers were, like their American counterpart, so called from their custom of dancing when moved by the Holy Spirit: their own name for themselves was the Children of God. Although at harvest time the men—mostly agricultural labourers—would work without pay for local farmers, the Establishment was resolved to be rid of them.

Some of their animals were confiscated on various pretexts, an attempt was made to have Mrs Girling certified insane, and when after three years they fell behind with their mortgage repayments there was an excuse to have them evicted. The *Hampshire Independent* reported: "The household goods were placed upon the high road with 2 or 3 pianos and harmoniums, 77 beds and bedding, farm produce, &c., supposed to be worth about £1,000. Then the inmates, numbering upwards of 140, including 40 children, were evicted. . . . There was a fierce east wind blowing with heavy rain and sleet and snow. The keen icy blast penetrated the thin dresses of the women and little ones. The furniture was soaked and spoiled. Hay, straw and beans were strewn about the road and the scene was one of terrible privation and desolation. After some hours of misery the children were removed to a neighbouring cottage".

The adults, who had grouped themselves round Mother Girling singing hymns, "appearing to regard their hard lot as only a portion of the persecution which those who are the Lord's must expect to undergo in this world", remained in the open all night, and "the morning found them half-perished with the bitter cold". Neighbours brought bread and cheese and milk, and in the evening further snow and a threat of being put in the Workhouse persuaded them to shelter in a barn. Somehow they regrouped themselves and managed eventually to lease a small farm at Tiptoe. Their leader died in 1886 and an account written a few years later observed: "As she had told her followers, and they believed, that she would never die, the event was a great shock to the faith of the 12 women and 8 men who remained with her to the last".

# Horndean ✑

It is only in recent years that the village has begun to spread out on either side of the turnpike road which gave it its existence in the 18th century—and, as the A3, contributed to its growth. The completion of the motorway to Portsmouth from the north will drive further into oblivion the most singular traffic link between the village and Portsea Island—the Portsdown and Horndean Light Railway, in effect a tram service via Cosham and Waterlooville, which opened in 1903 and closed in 1935.

The name of the village is known far afield, though concealed in the initials HSB, to enthusiasts of real ale. I was delighted to find Horndean Special Bitter on a recent visit to Berkshire, and amused to find a character in Julian Rathbone's 1980 novel *A Last Resort* consoling himself with the reflection that a "pub that serves Gale's beers can't be all bad. . . . Ern hated the club, but it was within walking distance and he loved Gale's beers." Now I see where the Horndean Light Railway went wrong: its tickets carried advertisements for Brickwood's.

# Hursley ✑

The present appearance and past history of the village are inextricably bound up with the fortunes of Hursley Park, which were at their highest when the village street along its eastern boundary was rebuilt with estate cottages. Their uniform appearance with latticed windows and Tudorish design reflects Edwardian prosperity.

It is, however, on the northern edge of the park that the remains of the earliest settlement may be seen. Merdon Castle was a Saxon encampment taken over by the Danes, and the site was then chosen for no obvious reason by Henry of Blois (see Bishop's Waltham) as one of the strongpoints, half castle and half palace, to be used in his brother King Stephen's wars against Empress Matilda.

It was abandoned in the 15th century when a hunting lodge was built roughly on the site of the present building. The Great

Lodge, its successor, was acquired by Oliver Cromwell's son Richard when he married the owner's daughter in 1649. He left her behind when he fled to France in 1660 but returned to this country and was buried in the church in 1712. When the Great Lodge was demolished a few years later the Great Seal of the Commonwealth was found hidden in a crevice.

The building had been sold by Cromwell's daughters to Sir William Heathcote, son of a Baltic merchant and later MP for Southampton: the mansion he built on the site is the nucleus of the present house. His son Thomas rebuilt the church in 1752. A descendant, another William, in 1836 appointed his Oxford tutor John Keble, founder of the High Anglican movement, to the living. Keble hesitated before accepting, but eventually stayed as rector for 30 years, rebuilding the church partly from the proceeds of his book of holy verse, *The Christian Year*. One of his best-known hymns, "Sun of my soul", is sung to the tune "Hursley".

The estate was acquired in 1902 by George Cooper, a Scottish solicitor who married an American heiress. They employed an army of workmen and a corps of artistic experts–Sir Joseph Duveen, for example—to modernise and extend the house and to build an entertainment annexe. This last was not only for the family's use. It was also made available—with free lighting, heating and staffing—for dances and other village functions: it was in effect a parish hall, and was even equipped with a projection-room, a stage, dressing-rooms—and a squash court. This was, as we have seen, something of a boom period for the whole estate.

But Sir George, as he had become in 1905, died in 1940 and the house was offered—as it had been during the First World War—for use as a military hospital. However, it was requisitioned by Lord Beaverbrook, then Minister of Aircraft Production, and handed over to Vickers-Armstrong, who had been bombed out of their Supermarine works at Southampton, and it was here that Spitfire modifications were planned and the engines tested.

Men of the British Eighth Division had camped in the park during the First World War; forty years later, the servicemen were American. My wife, who worked in the Vickers-Armstrong drawing office, was one of a group of natives who thereby learned the rudiments of baseball in their lunch-breaks. She still recalls various experiments undertaken by bored young draughtsmen who would rather have been on active service than placed compulsorily in a reserved occupation. These included feeding bullrush seeds into the ventilation system to see what would happen (they drifted in hundreds on to the drawing-boards like miniaturised parachutists), and attaching a half-inch paper aeroplane by a hair to a bluebottle to see whether it could be towed like a glider (it could).

Unconsciously this empirical approach echoed an experiment said to have been made a century earlier. A well in the park was reputed to be bottomless, but connected by an underground stream to a small pond, the Pole Hole, at Otterbourne a couple of miles away. Two ducks inserted at the former are reported to have emerged featherless at the latter; but this tale is no doubt a *canard*!

In 1958 Hursley park was acquired by the American computer firm IBM.

# Hurstbourne Priors ❧

Cobbett insisted on calling it Downhusband: for his beloved Uphusband, see the next entry. It is of course downstream from the latter, with the name Paper Mill Farm near the confluence of this particular bourne with the River Test as a reminder of a vanished industry.

In 1574 the Lord of the Manor, Sir Robert Oxenbrigge or Oxenbridge, Constable of the Tower of London, decreed that his executors should erect a tomb "suitable to his degree of a knight and with an epitaph thereon, ornamented with the insignia appertaining to his warlike career". At some point it was given a warlike camouflage of grey paint, and moved—but all was made good in 1964, when the proper colours were restored.

On the church bells there is the following inscription:

> I as treble surge
> I as second sing
> I as third ring
> I as truth sound
> I as tenor hum around

—a sort of station-identification followed by the announcement

> I to the church the living call
> And I to the grave summon all:
> Attend to the instruction which I give
> So that you may for ever live.

In 1662 the Dean and Chapter of Winchester were given permission to fell as many oaks as they required for the repair of the cathedral roof. Early in the next century, perhaps by way of compensation, avenues of oak, beech and horse-chestnut were planted. The Grange—its connection with the Priory of St Swithun and the diocese commemorated in the name Priors' Walk—was demolished in 1785 and its replacement destroyed by fire in 1890.

Common land at Hurstbourne Priors once totalled some 700 acres but now only 48 remain. The greater part was enclosed during the 19th century but during the last war 211 acres were commandeered for food production—and kept by the Ministry of Agriculture in 1952 after a compulsory purchase order. The parish council accepted £250 compensation to be put into a trust fund "for the benefit of the village and to protect what remains of the common".

# Hurstbourne Tarrant

The "Tarrant" is from the Dorset village of Tarrant Crawford, whose nuns owned land here. Both parish churches had murals depicting the Three Living (kings in their finery) and the Three Dead (skeletons).

Joseph Blount, Cobbett's friend, lived in a farmhouse by the bridge at the bottom of the hill which drops the Andover road into the valley of the Bourne. Pewter plates of pickled pork and potatoes (a mouthful in more senses than one) used to be set out on a low wall for wayfarers. Was Cobbett thinking of this, or Blount's hospitality at the termination of one of his "Rural Rides", when he particularly commended the village "on account of the excellent free-quarter that it affords"?

It was in any case, in Cobbett's estimation, "a sight worth going many miles to see" with its houses scattered about among fine and lofty trees. Laurence Vulliamy, whose photographic exploration *Rural Rides Revisited* beautifully contrasts then with now, records that Cobbett made no less than 29 references in his "Rides" to the village he knew and loved as "Uphusband".

As well as the hurdles turned out by craftsmen in so many Hampshire villages, Hurstbourne Tarrant specialised in the making of baskets and buckets and coops, or wooden casks. There was a coopers' club which held a Whit Tuesday procession round the village, ending in supper at the Coopers' Arms.

Anna Lea Merritt, the American-born painter whose "Love Locked Out" was bought for the Tate Gallery and came to epitomise one aspect of Victorian taste, moved to a thatched cottage—since demolished—at Hurstbourne Tarrant in 1891, partly in an attempt to recover from her deep grief at her husband's death. Her book about the village, *A Hamlet in Old Hampshire*, was published in 1902 with her own illustrations and is very much a period piece.

"All events from the outer world, our letters, our guests, descend as from beyond the sky, slowly and carefully", she wrote. "The traveller . . . sees the little village held as in the hollow of a hand, the ancient stone church shepherding the flock of homesteads and the crowded fold of those that sleep. Pious and blessed hands have recently saved the precious edifice from decay."

Mrs Merritt—she died in 1930—records how the shop-and-post-office was presided over by "the most dignified and orderly mistress", liable to be upset at the newcomer's preference for taking things straight home without their paper wrappings.

Children curtseyed and pulled their forelocks ("respect is especially pleasing when there is some doubt of deserving it") but grown-up visitors had "no topics, no books, no studies, no interests except the new vicar and the servant question". The American settler found problems of class in her English home quite baffling. "The degrees of social position are mysterious beyond comprehension", she wrote, instancing a neighbour who inadvertently opened her door to a workman and then sent a servant to see what he wanted. And, unlike their counterparts in the States, farmers did not themselves join in the ploughing or reaping.

In her day each cottager could pasture two cows on the 600-acre common at the top of the hill, and rent for 2s 7d a year an allotment 200 by 15 feet at the bottom. They were worked by men each evening after a ten-hour day, paid at the rate of 11s a week: then home to a tiny cottage crowded with eight or nine children—"Meat is certainly not tasted except on Sundays". The men were handsome, but lined and stiff at 40, liable to end their days breaking flints for road-mending.

Mrs Merritt's descriptions of adapting her city instincts to village life, and running her house and garden, deserve to take their place at the head of a procession of similar books which in recent years seem to have been published at the rate of two or three a week.

Another settler in Hurstbourne Tarrant who sometimes baffled the village was Mrs Doris Bladon-Hawton. Soon after the Second World War she established a craft gallery in a disused chapel. Later the "Bladon Gallery" spilled over into adjoining cottages and supported, one at a time, resident artists and craftsmen of various nationalities. One, Werner Haub, went on to run his own village gallery—Ash Barn at Stroud, near Petersfield.

Mrs Bladon-Hawton, who died in 1971, had great determination, a small smile, and a black dog called Arnold. "They think in the village", she told me one day displaying all three, "that I don't know that they call me Mrs Arnold".

# Hythe ✑

The name of the village means "landing-place", but there was little more than a sloping hard until an Act of Parliament authorised a jetty in 1844—a pier following in 1880. Between those dates the present ferry company began operations. A 2-foot gauge railway was laid along the pier in 1922, and in 1972 it was reported that the electric locomotives—built during the First World War for a factory making mustard gas—had been running for 50 years "at double their intended voltage with no trouble, a tribute to their original design".

Wherry and ferry brought over from Southampton most of the goods needed in Hythe and its hinterland until the coming in 1925 of the railway (see Fawley). It was not a separate parish of its own until the middle of the last century, and it is in the Fawley parish records for 1725 that we read that: "Charles Ivimey of Hieth, taken by pirates and carried captive by force, entered upon a brave resolution to destroy ye captain of ye pirates, which he attacked, and redeemed himself and his companions; but died at home of smallpox".

"Hythe is a hamlet on the other side of the Water," said an appeal published—presumably on the mainland—in 1840, "and nearly opposite to the town of Southampton; it is in the parish of Fawley, but separated from it by a part of Dibden, which surrounds it. It is five miles from its own parish church, is a place of resort from a great extent of country as a passage to and from Southampton, and has a large population of seamen, and others, who have long been prevented from divine service by the distance from the parish church and the want of accommodation therein."

St John's Church, erected in consequence, is both witness to the success of the appeal, and a memorial to the former brickworks in Claypits Lane, where there used to be a puddle-mill operated by a donkey.

A farm cottage in Jones Lane is reputed to be the oldest building in the village. In 1675 the rent was sixpence a year on the understanding that the tenant, Joan Bound, "did suit at the court of John Scullard as often as it should be held at Fawley". In the back garden a stone marked the boundary of the Cadland Estate to which most of the village belonged until 1895.

At a sale that year the police station fetched £234, top price being paid for the Drummond Arms which went for £3,550.

At the other end of the village The Travellers' Rest remained, as late as 1950, the sort of pub where the "public" had high wooden settles arranged round the walls and the "private" was in effect the landlord's sitting-room. If invited by Mr Snudden (he grew his own tobacco and wore a knitted hat of his own design), one sat on a chintz-covered sofa while he drew the beer from a barrel across the way.

Earlier, Hythe had had its own brewery in Langdown Lane. By the twenties it was disused, though as an old resident recently described, the vats in the cellar provided ideal sailing conditions for toy boats! Real boats were designed, made, tested and sailed—or driven—in the yards and the water near by, and T. E. Lawrence (alias Aircraftman Shaw) was involved in the development of high-speed rescue launches at the RAF base. Langdown House, built in 1800 by George Tate (he is commemorated by Tate's Road on the Langdown Estate) was demolished in 1963 after being used by BOAC in their bring-back-the-flyingboat era just after the Second World War; and by the Royal Navy—who sold it in 1961 for £30,000.

In 1977 died Richard N. Smith, grocer. He did his best to introduce a continental note to the village at the time of the vast residential expansion during the previous couple of decades, with his open-air refreshment stall and tables and chairs on the pavement. He used to walk down the High Street with a turkey feather on his head, and at election time presented his own version of a party political broadcast—gramophone records supporting the Conservative cause were played loudly just inside the window of a front room.

Another front room in Hythe which I used to visit 30 years ago was just inside a cottage door marked (one could specialise in those days!) "Sunday Newsagent". The papers were set out on a sofa in, whether deliberately or not, descending order of lewdness.

Twenty years ago, when Southampton Docks were extended to increase containerisation facilities, several acres of land were reclaimed on the western side of the Water. One unforeseen result was that a new site had to be found for the annual 20-minutes-each-way Football-In-The-Mud match between Hythe and Marchwood. It had been started in the 'thirties to raise funds for the Cottage Hospital and revived after the war in aid of various charities. The traditional "pitch" was beyond the end of the pier, but even at low tide the mud was not, by 1965, what it used to be. Fortunately a suitably glutinous area was found just south of the pier.

# Itchen Abbas 🍃

In the churchyard lies the body of John Hughes, rat-catcher and basket-maker. In 1825 a Judge at Winchester Assizes observed, in sentencing him to be hanged, "The crime of horse-stealing prevails to such an extent that it is absolutely necessary that the severest punishment should be inflicted to deter others from the commission". It seems to have had the desired effect since Hughes was the last man hanged for the offence in this country. Perhaps catching rats and making baskets had provided him with what today we should call a front, since he admitted at his trial that he had lived largely on the proceeds of crime.

Charles Kingsley (see Eversley) visited Itchen Abbas to fish "the loveliest of vale rivers" and stayed at The Plough: not the present building but its predecessor, which stood round the bend in the road towards Winchester. Though it was in his book *Hereward the Wake* that he pointed out that the waters of the Itchen were so clear that "none could see where water ended and where air began", the stream itself is described in *The Water Babies*. Tom, his little chimney-sweep, sees life on its bed through the eyes of newt, a precise and powerful act of imagination on Kingsley's part. His imagination was combined with the skill in observation which informs Janet Marsh's book on the Upper Itchen Valley (see Easton).

An earlier naturalist, Earl Grey of Fallodon, took refuge at Itchen Abbas from his parliamentary duties and hoped perhaps to forget the destruction by fire in 1917 of his family home at Fallodon. But in 1923 he received in London a letter from the woman who looked after his cottage saying: "My Lord, what can I say to you? I am sore vexed, but your pretty cottage is burned to the ground".

102

# King's Somborne 🐑

Ancient trackways on high ground are often called Oxdroves from the days when Welsh drivers used to take their cattle from the principality to fairs and markets in southern England (see East Woodhay and Stockbridge). King's Somborne has a modest version, the Cowdrove, which in one direction was used by travellers unwilling or unable to pay the tolls on the "new" turnpike road to Stockbridge. Another alternative was the lane through Houghton on the far side of the Test, but between village and river lay the high ground still marked on maps as "John of Gaunt's Deer Park". South of it the Romans had a river-crossing, and it is said that a camp site they established was used again for army manoeuvres some 19 centuries later, in 1935.

Ecclesiastically speaking, the village's history has been somewhat erratic. A bell used to be rung at nine on Sunday morning to tell the parish whether the parson had gone hunting or was at home. Somewhat later a man was nearly put in the stocks for preaching, although he had never been ordained; and the village school, opened in 1842, was hailed as the most successful National School in the county.

Perhaps the present Education Committee could get hold of a copy of a booklet written by the vicar of the time, the Reverend Richard Dawes, some ten years later and entitled *Hints On An Improved And Self-paying System Of National Education*.

When Cecil Bailey left the school in the 1950s his father, a local hurdle-maker, encouraged him to try his hand at the ancient craft. John Norwood tells his story in *Craftsmen at Work*. A lonely all-weathers job deep in the woods, it depends on buying each year a big enough area of coppice to provide the necessary raw materials. "At one time", says Mr Norwood, "lots were sold in the early autumn at a meeting in the clubroom of the Crown Inn, and each purchaser was required to have a bondsman, since payment was not made until cutting finished in the spring when the lots were measured. Around King's Somborne the coppices were parcelled into areas known as 'burls' which do not correspond to exact acreages."

Kingsclere– Half speed on the gallops.

# Kingsclere ✑

Six roads meet in the village. I suspect that nowadays each brings a fair proportion of Richard Adams' readers in search of Watership Down, high on the chalk escarpment which protects the village from the south more dramatically than do the wooded hills to the north.

William the Conqueror gave what had been a royal Saxon manor to Hyde Abbey, Winchester, but it was transferred in 1107 to the Canons of Rouen and its revenues—which earned it the label of the wealthiest benefice in the diocese of Winchester—helped to build Rouen Cathedral.

Cleanliness did not, in Kingsclere, come next to Godliness. King John stayed with the monks while hunting. He spent a most uncomfortable night, being badly bitten by bed bugs. The next morning, being "much impressed by the number and size of his bedfellows" he promised his hosts a weather-vane for their chapel. The vane on the steeple of the parish church today is a reminder that the royal gift, when it arrived, was in the form of a bug.

The Paulets, Marquises of Winchester, acquired the manor in Tudor times and the last official entrusted with the care of the deer in what had been for so many centuries a royal hunting preserve was Sir Henry Kingsmill. He died in 1625 and is commemorated by the marble and alabaster tomb his widow placed in the church in 1670. Kingsmills still farm near by around Ecchinswell.

The downs above the village echo the bloodstock country across the Berkshire border. At the end of the 19th century John Porter's stables produced six Derby winners—Blue Gown, Shotover, Blaise, Ormonde, Sainfoin, and Common. Today the stables of Ian Balding continue to train the finest racehorses. The most famous in recent years has been Mill Reef.

# Laverstoke 🦋

The village grew with Henry Portal's decision to move his paper-making business (see Overton and Whitchurch) upstream. The extent to which local people have been involved may be measured by the red-brick estate built in the middle of the last century for men working at the papermill—a "model village" widely known to students of planning and architecture.

In July 1873 a local newspaper story headed simply A GHOST stated: "A report that a mysterious being of this character pays nocturnal visits to the locality of Laverstock Mill has had the effect of drawing large numbers of credulous persons to the spot nightly during the week in the hope of having their spectral fancies gratified."

Somewhere in the churchyard lies the body of Thomas Langhorne Foster, who died at the age of 82 in 1930 after living for many years in a small square tower hidden in the woods between Laverstoke and Whitchurch. His rare callers were usually greeted by this solitary gentleman in his dressing-gown and with a loaded shotgun. In 1925 an intrepid salesman was allowed inside and, according to an account he wrote later, was informed that he was the first visitor to have crossed the threshold for several years. He noted a ceiling festooned with cobwebs and a wooden ladder by way of staircase. Bananas and onions lay in heaps on the floor. The salesman

105

recorded that he got his order—though his customer kept his shotgun at the ready throughout the interview.

The old church in Laverstoke Park (Laverstoke House was rebuilt at the end of the 18th century) became a private mausoleum for the Portal family, but it was demolished in 1952.

# Leckford 🦋

The Leckford Estate was bought by John Spedan Lewis in 1928. It was later enlarged, incorporating part of its twin village on the other side of the Test (see Longstock) and transferred to the department-store chain known as the John Lewis Partnership. Members of the stores' staffs (all known as "partners") have since then been able to make use of the facilities of both Leckford Abbas and Longstock Park, country mansions converted into guesthouses., The estate is believed to have been the first farm in the county to operate a five-day week.

# Lee-on-Solent 🦋

In 1236 Gilbert de Bret or Brut held the Manor of Ly. Unusually for these parts, his house was built of stone. Nevertheless it caught fire in the 14th century and a "temporary" home built for the family survives as the nucleus of Le Breton farmhouse in Manor Road. Until the coming of the railway—a three-mile branch from Fort Brockhurst opened in 1894—there were some four other buildings in Lee, and what did materialise never exactly came up to the expectations of various speculators who had envisaged a smart resort—or at least a popular seaside development. The tower at the point where the branch line terminated symbolised their high hopes and its use as an amusement centre long survived the railway, which carried its last passengers in 1930.

Forms of transport which were to have a less conventional effect on Lee were aircraft, naval and civilian, including helicopters and hovercraft. Some tricky legal problems of traffic priorities were posed by the construction of a hovercraft slipway across the shore road.

# Liphook 🖎

"So by coach to Lippock", wrote Samuel Pepys. "Here good honest people; and after supper, to bed." He was staying at The Crown, subsequently bought up and closed down by Mrs Elizabeth Keen, who ran a rival establishment, The Anchor. Patrons of this famous coaching inn included at various times not only George III and "Liberty" Wilkes, Nelson and Wellington, but also convicts due for transportation from Portsmouth who were chained up overnight in the cellars.

Liphook owes its existence to the London–Portsmouth road, and its 19th-century growth to the railway, which arrived in 1859—though only after frightful squabbles among the railway companies. The London and South Western, which served Portsmouth after a fashion with its line through Eastleigh (see Bishopstoke) to Gosport, never provided an express service on the "direct" and in 1865 ran only four passenger trains a day. It did not double the line until 1878. Nevertheless the arrival of the single line heralded, as elsewhere, the decline of the stagecoach—no longer would coaches pass through Liphook at the rate of one every hour. Their journey from London to Portsmouth took eight hours (this included a thirty-minute stop for refreshment at Guildford) and cost £1: the six hours to Liphook cost 13s 6d. The hamlet at which travellers then found themselves consisted of inns, farms, and a forge—all providing for wayfarers on what is now the A3. Some of them needed help from parish funds: one entry in the registers for the 18th century reads: "Give to 12 soldiers sick with ye smallpox, 2s."

Incidentally there were in Liphook others besides Pepys' "good honest people". A Women's Institute member is recorded in the WI anthology *It Happened in Hampshire* as stating that her grandfather—this would have been about 1840—and another man kept watch on a family grave for eight nights "for fear of body-snatchers".

Liphook is in the parish of Bramshott, so turn back to that entry for a rector's-eye-view of the "prevailing defects" of his parishioners in 1812!

# Liss ℘

Like Liphook, Liss seems to have had its naughty side. Place House, the site of a retreat for nuns from Winchester, appears to have been one of the first convents in the country to be suppressed.

Traditionally, a small boy from the village was regularly put in the oven of the Flying Bull. No suggestion of cannibalism, just an incident that was part of the ceremony of beating the parish bounds and owed its origin to the fact that the boundary was believed to pass through the kitchen of the inn.

In the 19th century an unusual crop was harvested in Liss in considerable quantities: peppermint. Several large beds were cultivated and the mint from them distilled and sold at four-pence a pint. How suitable that the family who made the mint was named Money!

# Longparish ℘

The obvious derivation is for once the right one. In fact it was orginally a nickname which came to supplant Middleton, the middle settlement (with 13th-century church), of a village having East Aston at one end and Forton at the other. The frequent right-angled turns of the single road which straggles through it along the Test valley for two miles mark old lanes which led up from the river through fields to Harewood Forest.

This was used during the Second World War for the storage of ammunition, which brought new life for a few years to an old branch railway connecting the London–Salisbury line at Hurstbourne station, near St Mary Bourne, with the Andover–Southampton line at Fullerton. Longparish Station was cut off from the village by the Andover–Salisbury road. The railway bridge was not demolished until 1960 when Royal Engineers from Barton Stacey blew it up so that the A303 could be widened. Passenger trains had been withdrawn as far back as 1931, though the line from Fullerton to Longparish was used for freight until 1956.

Opened as a double-track route in 1885, it was built largely for strategic reasons by the London and South Western in order to thwart the Great Western and its subsidiaries from providing through trains from Paddington to Bournemouth. Known for some reason as "The Nile", it was a favourite with Queen Victoria and she is said to have asked for royal trains to be routed this way between Windsor and Southampton when she visited her Isle of Wight retreat at Osborne. In the 1920s the track was used for the original (silent) film version of "The Ghost Train". The mailbag robbery scene was shot near Longparish Station, with Andover Fire Brigade providing "rain" from their hoses.

Far older than such johnny-come-lately activities as running railways, is the country craft of sedge-weaving (see Longstock). At Longparish it is still a cottage industry: the raw materials are readily available in the Test and, once the sedge is cut and drawn ashore, it is cleaned, dried, stored, dampened for use, plaited and made into attractive shopping baskets and tubs for logs.

R.Test at Longstock

# Longstock 🦢

The River Test, seen here at its finest (there are only minor variations in the quality of both angling and scenery), provided in earlier days a tempting route for various kinds of explorer whether he were primarily a raider or a settler. A wide artificial channel in the water-meadows here is believed to have been dug by Danish invaders for their flat-bottomed boats. The "dock" could have been something between a base-camp for further exploration and a "rail-head" through which supplies could be channelled to settlers or loot despatched home. The channel is 300 feet long and the excavated earth piled up to make a primitive quay.

Sadly there is no such evidence for the story that, at the time of the Danish raids, a horse with golden shoes was buried in a nearby wood named Money Bunt. It is hardly surprising that local children used to dig for the treasure from time to time— and they were no more successful than the villager who tried in vain to recover his savings from a roadside spot between Longstock and Stockbridge where he had buried them. He had dug a hole under a hedge after a friend had told him his money would be safer in a "bank" than in his cottage! When the time came to make a withdrawal he couldn't remember the right . . . branch?

A more successful digging operation is commemorated in the name of the village pub, the Peat Spade. Farmers used to allow their labourers one day off a year to cut the peat, and also allowed them to borrow a farm cart to take it home. As well as peat from sedge the valley once provided raw materials for the rush mats, baskets, and Moses cradles woven at Longstock up to the time of the Second World War.

Arthur and Ernest East, who inherited Longstock Park (see Leckford) when their father died in 1914, are buried in a small enclosure, marked by a holly hedge and an ash tree, at a spot which was their favourite viewpoint. Another death was recorded by a gypsy memorial cut in the turf at the side of the road where a little boy fell from a cart or caravan and was killed: passing gypsies long afterwards used to make sure that it was kept clear and white.

# Lyndhurst

Probably the most telling reminder of the village's history as the administrative centre of a royal hunting preserve is the

Tudor stirrup, used for the Norman device of expedition. If a dog was too big to pass through the expedition stirrup it was reckoned to be a risk to the king's deer, and its claws were maimed (expeditated) to prevent it being an effective hunter.

Stories of whole communities being wiped out by William the Conqueror to create his "New" Forest are usually discounted nowadays. As Desmond Hawkins points out in *Cranborne Chase* a forest—in its original sense of hunting preserve—was, in medieval times as in Africa today, an enormous larder of food on the hoof. Hunting was part of the economy: not, as he observes, just something the Plantagenets did at weekends because they had no golf courses.

The expedition stirrup is kept in the Verderers' Hall next to the Queen's House, a former royal hunting lodge and residence. It cost £2,000 to build in 1563 and £20,000 in 1966 to refurbish. The Verderers have managed the Forest—but not the forestry, that is the growing of timber—since the 14th-century. The Forestry Commission was established in 1919 after the Crown's timber interests had developed to the detriment of the commoners' rights. George Ryle comments in *Forest Service* that "there was constant friction between both sides right up until 1946". Since then the often conflicting interests of deer-management, timber-growing, and what is now known as leisure amenity have been reasonably well resolved apart from an occasional feeling that ordinary villagers are sometimes the last to be considered.

Originally, Lyndhurst was served by a chapel administered from the church of the parish, which was Minstead. The last chapel, built in 1740, was pulled down when Lyndhurst built its own church a century or so later. Noble by Victorian standards, it has William Morris windows and a fresco behind the altar by Lord Leighton which depicts the wise and foolish virgins. Which of the ladies, if any, were based on local models is still a matter of local debate.

Probably fewer visitors come to admire the church than to look in the churchyard for the grave of the original of Lewis Carroll's *Alice in Wonderland*. She was Alice Liddell, daughter of a classical scholar and wife of a gentleman-cricketer, Reginald Hargreaves (he played for Hampshire). They lived at Cuffnells, an 18th-century mansion described by a guidebook of 1801 as being notable for a conservatory "filled with a choice assemblage of indigenous and exotic plants". Occupied by the army during the Second World War, the house subsequently had a brief career as a hotel before being demolished in 1951.

While staying at Cuffnells, George III visited another 18th-century house at Lyndhurst, Netherwood. This has been converted into flats after being used for a time as a Forestry Commission training centre. Another big house, Vernalls, was at one time the home of Admiral Arthur Phillips (in 1788 he established at Sydney the first settlement on Australian soil), but the house was later pulled down to improve the entrance to nearby Brooklands. The admiral also rented "Glasshayes", so called from its extensive greenhouses. Later it became the Grand Hotel, a name changed recently to the New Forest Park.

A Tudor house originally inhabited by one of the royal forest keepers and known as Coxleys or Coxlease was transformed in Georgian times into a country house in the "Strawberry Hill Gothic" style by a friend of Walpole's. Now called Foxlease, it became in 1922 the Girl Guide movement's first training centre.

Parish registers show that in 1811 villagers were paid threepence a dozen for birds' heads (a primitive form of crop-protection) and fourpence a hedgehog; it was believed that hedgehogs helped themselves to milk from cows' udders.

In 1816, £1 18s 6d was spent on beer for those attending the parish meeting. Cutting peat to provide fuel for the poor cost 2s per thousand turves, but cartage cost 3s 6d per thousand.

By 1832 at the time of the agricultural depression—and rioting—the parish had 1,000 tickets printed and distributed among householders. The idea was that beggars and vagrants should each be given a ticket and told to report to the workhouse overseer, who was supposed to "relieve the vagrant according to his discretion". At the same time the parish limited his discretion somewhat by ordering that in each case the handout of bread should be limited to one pennyworth per vagrant.

Today most of the vagrants arrive in cars and caravans.

# Marchwood ✣

In May 1792 Marchwood Ladies Cricket Eleven, dressed in white with blue ribbons, were at home to Eleven Young Ladies of the Forest (their ribbons were green). The visitors won by 36 notches.

Marchwood girls also used to dress in white for the May Day celebrations. They went from house to house singing

> A branch of May we have brought you
> And at your door it stands:
> It's a very fine sprout
> And will spread about—
> It's the work of Our Lord's hands.

Seeing that the hedges did not sprout and spread about too much was the job of the village Hayward. In this century he was also responsible for straying cattle and ponies—he had no salary but was entitled to claim from owners whose animals he had impounded.

More impounding was done by the Revenue Men. Cracknore Hard was where the contraband was brought ashore, being the only place on a marshy shoreline where a boat could be safely beached. The last smuggler to be caught with his illegal cargo was arrested in 1873.

Machwood is possibly unique in having a swimming ghost. He is said to be the spirit of a soldier drowned while trying to escape arrest; he had fallen asleep while on guard duty and his nocturnal appearance is an action replay of his unsuccessful bid for freedom.

What he was supposed to be guarding is commemorated in the name "Magazine Lane". The armaments depot has intermittently caused anxiety among local people, especially in 1920 when "the whole sky was blushing red" as waste cordite was burned on the foreshore. In the Second World War Marchwood was, whether accidentally or otherwise, the first target in the Southampton area for German bombers. What became a military port continued to worry civilian authority, though the Ministry of Defence assured Southampton City Council in 1978 that there was "no real cause for apprehension from the danger of gunpowder stored in the magazine".

Among the actual residents of Marchwood more alarm seems to have been caused by the New Forest Council's determination to provide a site for gypsies on the edge of the village.

# Martin

When Cranborne Chase was a royal hunting preserve (later the rights of "vert and venison" devolved upon individual landowners), two of the king's foresters went to the house of John le Bor at Martin and took away an unnamed man, alleged to have broken the forest laws, to Cranborne. There they hanged him without reason ("unjuste suspenderunt")—subsequently confiscating two oxen they said belonged to le Bor. Today preservation in Martin means something different, to the point where the county council's policy of keeping new building to a minimum has led to claims that it is resulting in "moribundity". Also, perhaps, to the award in 1978 of the title of Hampshire's best-kept village (by then it had on four occasions been the runner-up).

In 1226 Martin had its own Wednesday market—the old drovers' road along the top of the downs being conveniently near by. Martin Down itself was, eight and a half centuries later, declared a nature reserve largely because of its rare acreage of unploughed downland. This was a stretch of countryside the writer-naturalist W. H. Hudson knew well and in the churchyard there is a memorial to Shepherd Lawes, the original of "Isaac Balcombe" in Hudson's book *A Shepherd's Life*.

# Micheldever ✎

William Cobbett called Micheldever Forest "one of the finest oakwoods in Britain". Not only has a Roman villa been unearthed in the wood but archaeologists who mounted a rescue operation in the path of the M3 motorway found traces of still earlier occupants in an oval-shaped barrow used as a Bronze Age burial site.

The name of the village means either much or marshy water, and the stream called the Dever used to be more simply known as the Northbrook. The triangular area in the middle of the village known as "The Crease" is probably derived from the cross where four lanes meet.

In November 1703 there was a terrible three-day storm in which a chimney crashed through the roof of East Stratton House and the occupant, Lady Rachel Vaughan, recorded: "My farms are torn to pieces, corn and hay may be seen hanging from the trees, Hampshire is all in desolation."

East Stratton House was acquired in 1740 by Francis Baring, founder of the banking firm of Baring Brothers: his father had been a clothmaker in Devon and his grandfather, Franz, a Lutheran pastor in Bremen. During the Agricultural Riots of 1831 William Baring had his hat knocked off by a 19-year-old ploughboy, Henry Cooke, who was subsequently found guilty of attempted murder; hanged at Winchester; and buried at Micheldever in an unmarked grave on which, according to legend, the snow never settled. The Baring family vault is inside the church, but no trace remains of the graves either of Cooke or of "Savage Bear", who sounds like an Indian brave but who was said—according to a headstone erected in 1813—to have come from Hursley.

In 1917, seven lead coffins were found under the stokehole of the church. In 1963 one which was accidentally broken open—it measured 7 by 3 by 2½ feet—was found to be packed with peat: an attempt, perhaps, to preserve a body on a long journey.

Two miles northward the settlement of Micheldever Station grew up when the London and Southampton Railway was built in 1840. The station was known as "Andover Road" until the line to Andover—ten miles away—and Salisbury was built.

# Milford 🙎

There was little more than a hamlet at Milford when Colonel Cornwallis West inherited Newlands Manor in 1886. His ambition was to do what his friend the Duke of Edinburgh was doing at Eastbourne, that is to create a fashionable seaside resort practically from scratch. About all that happened, however, was that a Milford Improvement Committee was formed. It organised a public subscription to provide a golf course, a cricket ground, and seats and shelters overlooking the sea. Even then it remained, until half a century ago, what one resident called "a real village"—connected, she said, to Lymington only by two buses of which one was known affectionately as The Hearse and the other The Rabbit Trap.

The Colonel's Newlands Manor became mildly famous as an example of Gothic Revival. An odd link with 20th-century showbiz was unintentionally formed by a relative, Mrs Whitby, when a silken banner she had made was acquired in a sale by the manager of the Rialto Cinema in Southampton and exhibited in his foyer. An inscription below the 15-foot showcase explained that the banner was the "result of experiments in the culture of the silkworm of the Philippine mulberry, *morus multicantis*, during 14 years by Mrs Whitby of Newlands in the County of Hants" and was exhibited "in the desire of her survivors to hold up to honourable example a lady whose energetic perseverance strove to compass a labour of public utility". I wonder how much impression the result made on cinema-goers intent on such treats as drinks-on-a-stick and "Abbott and Costello meet Old Mother Riley"?

On the shingle spit which the tides piled up east of Milford Henry VIII used stones from Beaulieu Abbey to build Hurst Castle as part of his coastal defences. It became a maximum security prison for Charles I before his execution, Cromwell's advisers having suggested that Carisbrooke Castle on the Isle of Wight, where he had been held for a year, offered too great a risk of escape.

116

# Milton 🦋

Bunny is a Hampshire dialect word for a culvert (see Beaulieu) or ravine: Beckton Bunny and Chewton Bunny both provided such excellent routes for smuggling contraband that in 1837 the Revenue posted a Riding Officer to Milton, installing him in a cottage from which he could—in theory—keep an eye on both bunnies simultaneously. The coastal development which has since taken place along the stretch of shore between the two outlets is now Barton on Sea.

Perhaps the arrival of the Revenue Man and his activities had a greater effect than either he or his superiors had had in mind, since a guide published in the following year reported that "the improved morals of the district have attracted several visitors to the coast this summer".

The better class of visitor might well have been attracted to the social goings-on at the Gothic castle, built a few years previously at Highcliffe by Lord Stuart de Rothesay. His wife had infinitely preferred the original modest villa and was scandalised by the castle's cost: "When I think it is for this we are ruined, I wish the whole thing had fallen over the cliff", she complained. Instead it survived long enough to be engulfed by a tide of mid-20th century housing estates—though in the intervening period it was rented by the department-store pioneer Gordon Selfridge, who is buried in Highcliffe churchyard.

## Minley (see Yateley) 🦋

117

R.C.G. · Minstead Church

# Minstead ✺

Few settlements in the New Forest provide traces of prehistoric man: the poor soil was no incitement to give up a nomadic life in favour of settling down and growing crops. This is another reason to doubt whether the Norman kings ever indulged in wholesale clearances to establish a hunting preserve (see Lyndhurst). There was no need.

But the encampment on the site known as Malwood Castle (its present occupiers, the Southern Electricity Board, seem to prefer Castle Malwood) above the village of Minstead is an exception–Ancient Britons were here. So in due course was William Rufus, and one of those unverifiable legends says that somebody tried to spoil his hunting breakfast by warning him of his impending fate. Perhaps a ghostly voice harked back to the old religion, and forward to the best-seller, with the simple observation that The King Must Die. A few hours later, die he did, a little way away in Canterton Glen, whether by accident or design. His death from Walter Tyrrell's arrow is still marked

118

by a stone erected in 1745 by Lord Delawarr, who claimed he had seen the tree beneath which the Red King was shot. In fact, the stone itself is not there at all any more. It was encased in iron to protect it from souvenir hunters—but apparently in vain: when the casing was removed during an official inspection a few years ago, workmen discovered that there was nothing inside.

It's a pity that Sherlock Holmes was never called in to investigate this Case of the Missing Memorial. His creator, Conan Doyle—who had used the forest as a setting for much of his early historical novel, *The White Company*—bought a house in the parish at Bignell Wood a few years before his death, and is buried—"patriot, physician and man of letters"—in the churchyard.

The church itself, one of only two in the forest to be listed in the Domesday Book, has been altered and added to over the centuries (fortunately in the 17th and 18th rather than the 19th), just as a manor or farmhouse might have been. Private boxes, with seats rather than pews (one even has its own fireplace) were installed for the gentry; there is a double row of galleries, one above the other for more ordinary folk; and a three-decker pulpit ensures that somebody can always keep an eye on the congregation whoever may be preaching or reading the lesson.

The manicured appearance of the village indicates that Minstead boasts not merely clusters of thatched cottages but many a det. period res. in a much favoured (some house agents prefer sought-after) locality. The coming of the motorway to Cadnam has increased its accessibility and upped the prices. But perhaps you'd expect to pay a lot of money in a village that means the place of the mint!

# Monxton 🌿

The process of gentrification has gone even further at Monxton than at Minstead, and an old resident of Monxton complained to the *Evening Echo* in 1971 that: "It's all Air Vice Marshals and Brigadiers now." The reporter was told that by then there were only two villagers left: Mrs Win Locke and, next door to her in his father's shoe-maker's shop, Mr Victor Russell. Their father had bought both cottages when they, together with others, were sold by King's College, Cambridge, landlords since the 15th century. But three-quarters of the way through the 20th century, there was only one farmworker left in the village.

One wonders what his predecessors made of the Reverend Thomas Rothwell, who was theoretically in charge of the parish from 1723–48. He was "a most singular rector" who would sit alone in his parlour, to which his family were forbidden entry, and occupy himself with mathematics and algebra. For many years he "stirred not out of his house, no not even to Church, but had a constant curate though the Church is not a stone's throw from the rectory, and gave himself not time to be shaved, but let his beard grow till he was a spectacle".

So, presumably, he never saw the wayfarers whose passage through his parish was noted in the register for July, 1730: "Gave a parcel of slaves that came from Turkey, 1s."

# Morestead

Eggs at Christmas and strawberries on St John's Day: these were the dues of the Manor of Morestead in the 13th century to the Priory of St Swithun at Winchester, four miles away on the Roman road which now peters out south of the village. But the manor would have been hard put to find anything to send the prior a hundred years later, when the village lay devastated with most of its cottages in ruins in the aftermath of the Black Death.

The isolation of this downland settlement was one reason for its choice as the site of the camp built at Hazeley Down during the First World War for German prisoners. In the Second World War a German aircraft was shot down near by and its crew taken prisoner.

# Nether Wallop (see The Wallops)

120

# Netley Abbey

Should it really be Letley? The abbey, now in ruins, was founded in 1239 by monks from Beaulieu, the fine or beautiful place, *bellus locus*. *Laetus locus*, the happy place, may have been their name for their new foundation. In 1967 divers from a sub-aqua club were reported to be investigating treasure dumped in a pond by the monks "during the Norman invasion" (i.e. 175 years before the abbey was even built). Had they found anything it might possibly have been hidden at the time of the Dissolution in 1536.

The gatehouse of the abbey became the nucleus of Netley Castle (see below) but the main building, acquired by the Marquess of Winchester, passed in the 18th century to Sir Berkeley Lucy. Some of the materials were taken to Cranbury Park (see Otterbourne) to transform an estate cottage into a sham ruin: but the main contract for demolition went to a Southampton builder, Walter Taylor. He dreamed that the keystone of the west window fell out and fractured his skull. He was advised by Isaac Watts' father, to whom he reported the nightmare, not to proceed. However, he decided to take the risk, whereupon he was duly hit on the head by a piece of falling masonry. He died when an instrument the surgeon was using to extract a splinter of stone penetrated his brain.

Seeing, some years later, what was left of the abbey, Walpole observed that the ruins were not of Netley but of paradise. The poet Gray thought that the effect was greatly enhanced by the ivy. Today the remains are now officially an Ancient Monument with the accent on preservation rather than romanticism. It makes an effective background for open air theatricals; I remember a production of the miracle play "Everyman" punctuated by hollow slaps which were not a slow handclap from a restive audience, but attempts by members of the cast to free themselves from the mosquitoes which had swarmed in for an unexpected treat as the shadows lengthened.

The Tudor Castle was garrisoned against invaders from the Continent until 1627. In 1560 Queen Elizabeth slept there. So, in due course, did Baden-Powell, though by this time it had become a Victorian mansion in private ownership and the owner, Colonel Crichton, had invited the Baden-Powells to be

121

his guests during their honeymoon. It was later bought by Middlesex County Council and subsequently used for hospitals of various kinds.

Which brings us to Netley Hospital. It was built when the War Office belatedly realised, as a result of the Crimean War, that existing military hospitals were inadequate. The site was chosen so that casualties could be landed directly from troopships (the hospital pier was demolished in 1955).

Queen Victoria laid the foundation stone in 1856. In 1966 a reader of the *Southern Evening Echo* recalled how her grandmother who died in 1937 at the age of 92, walked all the way from Hamble to see the Queen—and was disappointed that she was such a tiny woman, and was not wearing a crown.

Florence Nightingale is usually credited with having persuaded the Government to build Netley. However, according to Lytton Strachey, when she belatedly saw the plans she discovered they "reproduced all the worst faults of an out of date system of hospital administration". Living near Romsey at Embley Park, Florence enlisted the help of her neighbour at Broadlands, Lord Palmerston. Accordingly he wrote to the War Office asking for building operations to be suspended because "the comfort and recovery of the patients have been sacrificed to the vanity of the architect, whose sole object has been to make a building which should cut a dash when looked at from the Southampton River".

The War Office, however, employed delaying tactics so successfully that Palmerston's interest evaporated and building went ahead. Constructed largely of bricks made from clay on the splendid 227-acre site fronting the east bank of Southampton Water, it was opened in 1863 and by 1870 could accommodate 1,400 patients in 138 wards. The corridors, a quarter of a mile in length, were on the south or seaward side of the building, so that the wards had the minimum of sunshine— the origin, no doubt, of persistent rumours that the monstrosity had been designed for New Delhi and that owing to a mix-up at the War Office India got the building that had been intended for Hampshire. A less catastrophic mistake proposed as an alternative theory is that the hospital was merely erected back to front!

122

In 1918 workers at Thornycroft's Woolston shipyards marched in protest to Netley because they believed that German prisoners of war were being treated in hospital beds while British soldiers were in tents in the grounds. No such misunderstandings seem to have occurred in 1944 and 1945 when the hospital was occupied by the American army.

After the war it was used for convalescents and a separate psychiatric unit continued to operate. Various ancillary buildings were built in the grounds. Chelsea Pensioners came down in batches for a breath of sea air. Hearing that they included some Boer War veterans, the BBC sent me along with a tape-recorder. Alas, by the time I got there they had returned to Chelsea and the new intake seemed to consist of veterans in the same Dad's-Army age-group as myself. . . .

The hospital was closed in 1955, survived a fire in 1963 and the investigations of sundry ghost-hunters for a decade. It was demolished—except for the chapel—in 1966. It now seems that the surviving buildings, which include a three-storey officers' mess of Italianate style, will mostly be used for police training, and that the grounds will be used partly as a nature reserve ("I see, Sir—investigating the natural habitat of the Nightingale down there in the bushes, were we?") and partly as an open space. In fact Hampshire County Council, which bought the site for £890,000, has officially designated it a "country park".

There remains a minor problem of erosion and responsibility. When the local authority asked for a grant towards maintaining the coastline, the Department of the Environment tartly replied that the area "falls below latitude 50, 50 degrees north, and does not count as coast at all". And the reply from the Countryside Commission to a similar request was that the area "could not be considered as countryside". But, unlike the DoE, the commission soon appeared to be capable of second thoughts.

Near Nomansland—

# Nomansland

The doorstep of the village pub is in Hampshire, so Nomansland is included in this book even if the pub is over the border in Wiltshire. Anyhow, Nomanslanders who die in Wiltshire are liable to be buried in Hampshire and cricket balls hit for six are seldom Wiltshire matters.

In 1750 Gypsy Willett found some land which belonged, apparently, to no man, and built a cabin or hut or hovel underneath the branches of an oak: and for years the area had the reputation of being happily free of landlords and other inconveniences such as rates and tithes. Settlers claimed "keyhold tenure" under which you could lay claim to your own patch so long as you could build your house in one night and have smoke coming out of the chimney by first light (today the existence of a chimneystack, even without a dwelling attached, is useful to anyone applying for permission to build).

In the middle of the last century a local character known variously as Dan Winter, or Hodder, or simply the Marquis, was the subject of a rhyme:

> Who lays here, who d'yer think?
> Old Dan Hodder, gained some drink.

Drink for a dead man? Aye! For Why?
While alive he was always dry.

It must have been in Dan's time or soon after that the first collector of the Poor Rate came to Nomansland. The oldest inhabitant, George King, refused to pay up: authority confiscated his clock.

Somehow one landowner, Mrs Sarah Chapman, had in 1855 four acres which were "extra-parochial" and so, as the only resident, she paid the county rate only. But 15 years later the world was beginning to impinge on Nomansland with the establishment of a village school designed by Giles Gilbert Scott, who also perpetrated St Pancras Station and the Albert Memorial.

The village still retains a slightly impromptu air, as though the older buildings might at any moment pick up their footings and scurry across the cricket pitch into the New Forest—leaving the incongruous grid of new houses where they belong, in Wiltshire.

# North Baddesley 🦡

The Black Death resulted not only in the depopulation of the countryside and the complete abandonment of a number of settlements but, for those who had the means, a move to a new site. The Knights Hospitallers of Jerusalem, driven by the plague from their quarters at Godsfield, near Alresford, established their chief commandancy for the Hampshire area at North Baddesley, on the site later to be occupied by the Manor.

At the dissolution of Romsey Abbey the beneficiaries were Thomas Foster of Baddesley Manor and his son, of whom it was written

> Mr Forster of Badsley was a good man
> Before the marriage of priests began,
> For he was the first that married a nun;
> For which he begat a very rude son.

Though housing estates have now all but submerged the old village it is not long since the area consisted of open fields and woods. A gravestone erected to Charles Smith says that he "suffered at Winchester on the 23rd March 1822 for resisting by firearms his apprehension by the gamekeeper of Lord Palmerston when found in High Coppice looking after what is called game, aged 30 years. If thou seest the oppression of the poor, and violent perverting of judgment, marvel not at the matter; for He that is higher than the highest regardeth, and there be higher than they".

However, there is another side to the picture. Lord Palmerston, whose estate at Broadlands then included High Coppice, asked for mercy for Smith. A sort of correction-stone was set up in 1906 which adds: "Charles Smith was convicted at Winchester Assizes of attempting to murder. A watcher named Robert Snellgrove approached Smith to identify him. Snellgrove, quite a youth, was alone and unarmed; Smith, with a companion and armed, fired at close range the whole contents of his gun at Snellgrove's body. In 1822 attempt to murder was a capital crime. Copies of the original papers connected with the case are deposited in the church chest".

## North Warnborough (see Odiham) ꙮ

# Oakley ꙮ

At the beginning of the century Oakley, now something of a dormitory for Basingstoke, was "a parish of 303 souls". In 80 years the population has swollen to over 4,000. I wonder how many of the newcomers have seen the lady who used to run up to riders in Shearsdown Lane, peer into their faces, and then vanish?

Perhaps she was looking for someone from the village who never returned from what seems to have been an anti-invasion exercise during the Napoleonic Wars. One version of the story is that all the able-bodied men—and women—from the parish were given scarlet uniforms and taken to line the Solent shore in an effort to suggest that the coast was efficiently defended.

126

Apparently they hadn't so much as a musket between them. Except for the colour of the uniform and the presence of the ladies it sounds a bit like the early days of the Home Guard: but why just Oakley? I'd be interested to hear of similar stories from other villages.

A century ago Oakley was one of the places where the Harvest Home was celebrated with due ritual. Workers on the Malshanger estate, wearing buttonholes of oats, wheat, barley, and rye tied in red ribbon, marched in procession to church for a harvest festival service followed by parish supper in the rectory barn.

# Odiham 🦜

Basingstoke has lost and Andover is losing what Odiham still retains: a sense of historical identity. Not being on a main road or railway has proved its saving. The Basingstoke Canal (see Greywell) had a short-lived effect. The wharves by the hump-backed bridge covered 3 acres, and were where chalk and farm produce were loaded, and coal was brought in. A revival of interest in the canal, now in the joint care of the Hampshire and Surrey County Councils, is echoed in the renaming of a nearby pub after a narrow-boat which used to work the canal: The Cricketers has become The Waterwitch.

The canal cut through the outer defences of King John's Castle, built in 1212 of stone and flint. It was from here three years later that he set out (by some accounts in a foul temper) for Runnymede and the signing of the Magna Carta. In 1216 the castle held out for a fortnight, though garrisoned only by three officers and ten men, against a French expeditionary force headed by the Dauphin. In 1232 the castle was given to Eleanor, sister of Henry III and wife of Simon de Montfort. Some centuries later, incidentally, her household accounts turned up in a French monastery: they showed that the going rate for fat hens at Odiham in the middle of the 13th century was two a penny. Later King David Bruce of Scotland was imprisoned in the castle for ten years.

Shortly after the Second World War there was a scheme to turn the castle grounds into a tea-garden but the threat was averted and in 1961 the parish council acquired the grounds and the ruins on payment of £10 legal fees. One councillor revealed that local children had particularly asked him to make sure the castle was not tidied up: it must have made a splendid adventure playground.

However, within five years the council was trying unsuccessfully to unload the ruins on the Ministry of Public Buildings and Works. Eventually, in 1971, Hampshire County Council agreed to take over and spend £4,000 on, I fear, tidying it up.

In 1788 the Humphries-Mendoza prizefight for the championship of England took place in a meadow at Palace Gate Farm, an event commemorated in numerous ways including the manufacture of ceramic figures and the writing of a satirical ballad, the Odihad. The spectators included the Prince of Wales.

Humphries, the winner, sent a message to his patron: "Sir, I have done the Jew and am in good health." Mendoza's supporters released a black pigeon, signifying defeat, to carry the news to his home in Whitechapel. A "hawk-nosed brilliant-eyed young man whose black hair hung in ringlets", he was the great-great-great-great-grandfather of Peter Sellers. A print showing the famous prize-fight which used to hang in the White Hart was presented to the parish council by the brewers when they closed down the inn in 1961.

French soldiers returned to Odiham during the Napoleonic Wars—as prisoners (see Bishops Waltham). One is buried beneath a stone inscribed "Death hath set him free". Their camp was in a big chalkpit on the Alton road. A mile along the road to Winchfield was Frenchman's Oak, the limit of the territory in which they were allowed to promenade. It has been suggested that they provided, voluntarily or otherwise, parties of men to work on the canal.

Owing to a shortage of copper coinage between 1775 and 1797 the canal contractors paid their men in shilling tokens which showed a spade and mattock in a wheelbarrow on one side and a sailing barge on the other. These did not have to be exchanged at a "company store" but were accepted at various public houses including the George at Odiham—which, with the King's Arms, was by 1964 all that remained of seven licensed premises in the High Street (altogether the number of pubs in Odiham and North Warnborough has dwindled "within living memory" from 22 to 9).

In 1638 a London merchant, Sir Richard Gurney, gave at the request of his wife the leaseholds of several acres of gravel-pits and market gardens in West London to provide funds for the poor of Odiham, his wife's home. The leases, which expired only 20 years ago, were in the area of what is now Hammersmith Broadway: the proceeds were devoted to the building of almshouses. Their predecessors included May's Model Cottages, erected by a local wine-merchant in 1862. In 1962 one of the occupants received a visit from a 95-year-old man whose grandchildren had driven him to Odiham to see the house where he had been born.

In the same year died Miss Amy Clutton, who in 1936 had bought the Mill House at Pilcot Mill on the River Hart, which had a 15-foot waterwheel and was mentioned in the Domesday Book. Somewhat of a recluse, she had an edgy manner which "masked a truly charitable personality".

The RAF established itself at Odiham as early as 1925, somewhat to the alarm of various self-appointed guardians of public morals. One landowner asked the Commanding Officer to confine his airmen to the airfield so that the young ladies of the neighbourhood were not corrupted. Whether confinements of any kind ensued I have no idea.

The police may have felt they had more pressing problems to deal with, even in those security-unconscious days. One involved a 20-stone officer who, unable to open up the front door of the 200-year old police station, had himself hoisted by the breakdown crane from a nearby garage over a high wall at the back into a courtyard which he knew contained an unlocked entrance to the building. A young colleague is reported to have tactlessly pointed out that the front-door key was always left hanging on a string which could be hauled out through the letterbox. He probably gave up all chance of promotion by further demonstrating, when irascibly told that the string had broken, that the key could easily be extracted through the gap under the door.

In 1961 the station coach-house, where a horsedrawn Black Maria had originally been kept, was made into an interview room. One presumes that by then the practice of leaving suspects—or at least wrongdoers—to cool off outside the police station in the stocks had long been abandoned.

Dovecote, Old Basing House. R.C.G.

# Old Basing 🦢

"Whoever will come for brick or stone shall freely have the same for his pains": and Cromwell's invitation to the villagers to help ensure that Basing House was "slighted utterly" resulted in many buildings in Old Basing incorporating a chunk or two of solid history into their walls or foundations.

Originally a fortified house with a moat, Basing House was the administrative headquarters of Hugh de Port's vast Norman holdings in what had been the Saxon kingdom of Wessex. In Tudor times the Marchioness of Winchester, John Paulet's second wife, described it as being "in forme circular, encompassed with a brick rampart lyned with earth and a very deep ditch, but dry". William, the fourth Marquis (he married Lucy, daughter of one of the Cecils) entertained Queen Elizabeth so lavishly that it nearly bankrupted him.

John, the fifth Marquis, refortified the house during the Civil War and in 1643 held out with 300 men for six months against General Waller's Parliamentarians. But Cromwell, for whom the tide of battle had turned (see Cheriton), brought up the artillery that had battered Winchester into submission and the siege became another Roundhead victory.

The result seems to have been due more to the artillery which Cromwell brought up and placed under his personal command than to treachery and defection—though some of the defenders are known to have gone over to the enemy, and there is evidence that in the early stages of the siege the intentions of the Royalists were leaked to their besiegers.

A report in *The Kingdome's Weekly Post* described the final assault: "Immediately the dreadful battery began the great guns discharged their cholerick errand with great execution; many wide breaches were made in an instant, and the besieged immediately marshalled themselves, and stood like a new wall to defend those breaches; our men in full bodies and with great resolution came on. The dispute was long and sharp, the enemy, for aught I can learn, desired no quarter, and I believe that they had little offered to them. You must remember what they were. They were most of them Papists, therefore our musquets and swords did show but little compassion."

However, Cromwell's men did take between two and three hundred prisoners. Among them was the architect Inigo Jones, then in his seventies—carried out in a blanket because the Puritan soldiers had stripped him of his fine clothes.

The Marquis was sent to the Tower but allowed to take refuge in France, returning only at the Restoration. The house was destroyed partly by a fire that broke out after the attack and partly by deliberate "slighting" later.

The siege is recalled by the name Oliver's Delve, a chalkpit where Cromwell's pikemen and troopers dug themselves in, and by Slaughter Close; and by scars from cannon-shot on farm buildings. Cannon-balls, swords, and other items of military equipment were discovered when the Basingstoke Canal was dug a hundred years later. The octagonal dovecot of Basing House survived not only the battle but the operations of the canal "navigators". During the canal's comparatively brief existence it was a familiar towpath landmark for the bargemen. Admired nowadays for its elegant 16th-century brickwork, it was an eminently practical larder whose hundreds of inhabitants helped to eke out the menu during the lengthy siege.

The canal (see Odiham and Greywell) gave Basing a wharf: but the London and Southampton Railway (as it was called before the directors changed it to London and South Western to appease potential customers at Portsmouth) cut straight through the middle of the village on an embankment without so much as a halt. The physical division remains, more obtrusive than the sociological one which results from Old Basing having to be two things at once—a village in farming country and a commuter community.

# Otterbourne 🦎

"Woad still grows in the lanes", observed the Victorian writer Charlotte Yonge in *Old times in Otterbourne*, when she devoted her talents to the village where she had been born in 1823 and where she lived all her life.

By the middle of this century the fate of her original home, Otterbourne House (she lived later at " Elderfield") was in considerable doubt but in 1978, to provide it with a "last chance", permission was given to convert it into five flats.

Miss Yonge is buried near the church, which her father and John Keble (see Hursley) designed. In the course of her writings—Keble was one subject, the surrounding countryside another—she mentions a number of old traditions. One was "gooding": on St Thomas's Day "each poor housemother can demand sixpence from the well-to-do towards her Christmas dinner", though from Hursley in 1980 Miss G. A. Morrant recalled for me how her mother, then in her teens, had been persuaded by a friend to call on Miss Yonge one Gooding Day—but was turned away empty-handed when she gave her name and address. "I don't give my sixpences to people who live on the Hill", she was told: "they are the people I call the Proud Poor". Nevertheless Miss Morrant treasures her childhood memories of Otterbourne when "life was so different—happier and more sociable—and even being poor and miles from the town wasn't noticed because there were things like Penny Readings (socials), and people were real neighbours".

In 1973 a member of the Winchester Morris Men recalled how his great-uncle, Tom Goodchild, had belonged to the Otterbourne Mummers (see Boldre) in 1904 or 1905—a year or two after Charlotte Yonge's death—and had played, as a ten-year-old boy, the part of Little Johnny Jack. This is the character who normally makes the begging-speech, for it must be remembered that at least by late Victorian times the primary object of the mummers was to raise money for themselves and their families, rather than re-create a quaint folk-memory of the Crusades. Tom saw two revived versions of the play, one presented at Bitterne and the other by the New Forest Mummers: his verdict was that they hadn't taken the play seriously enough. But John Edgar Mann, to whom I am indebted for information on mummers throughout these pages, tells me that the veteran player did approve of the version presented at Otterbourne by his great-nephew's group.

Isaac Newton died at near by Cranbury Park, the home of his son-in-law and one-time pupil John Conduitt, where he had lived for the last 20 years of his life. Conduitt sold the mansion in about 1730 to Thomas Dummer, who thought that a pleasant embellishment to the Park would be the medieval Butter Cross from Winchester. The Corporation agreed to sell, but Dummer's men were driven off by irate apprentices who, with a greater respect for history than their masters, had appointed themselves an unofficial preservation group. Instead, Dummer acquired some stone from Netley Abbey (see Netley) and created a sham ruin behind which an estate cottage was to be hidden.

# Over Wallop (see The Wallops) 🎵

# Overton 🎵

Ten years ago a parish councillor recalled how in 1936, as an out-of-work electrician from Wales, he arrived at Overton under an employment scheme sponsored by Portals and asked how far their paper mill was from the station. "If you don't know how far it is", he was told, "you must be a stranger. We don't want any here so you'd best clear off and go back where you came from."

Fortunately, before long he was as well integrated as that earlier "stranger" who founded the firm had become within a few years of settling in England. Henri de Portal, a Huguenot escaping from religious persecution, landed at Southampton and found refuge with the French Protestant community settled round the church of St Julian. He was given employment in a paper mill on the Itchen north of the town at Stoneham, and within a year was naturalised as Henry Portal of South Stoneham, gentleman.

In 1710 a local landowner, Sir William Heathcote (see Hursley) offered him the lease of a mill on the Test (see Whitchurch). Later he acquired his own (see Laverstoke), and consolidated his English position by marrying Miss Dorothy Hasker of Overton. His contract of 1724 to produce notes for the Bank of England was no doubt facilitated by the fact that its Governor was Heathcote's uncle. Similar work for customers world wide resulted in considerable expansion and a move to Overton.

The original village was on the north bank of the river which explains why the church seems to some extent cut off from the village is serves. In the 13th century, de Lucy, Bishop of Winchester, laid out—as he did at "New" Alresford—a new settlement, on the south bank. When William of Wykeham was bishop a man who sought sanctuary in the church after accidentally killing someone was dragged out again by angry villagers, but His Lordship insisted on a proper inquiry instead of rough justice. Incidentally in case you find on an old map a nearby hamlet marked "Southampton," the name was later changed to Southington.

# Owslebury

Some people believe that the name of the village is derived from "ouse", a word for water which survives in the name of a number of rivers—but the theory doesn't, well, hold water any better than the chalk upland on which the settlement sits. A clue lies in the fact that the first two syllables are pronounced to rhyme with bustle rather than bamboozle. The most likely derivation is that it was a fortified place belonging to Osla.

Later it belonged to the Seymours, lords of the manor of Marwell. One incumbent of the parish cursed Sir Henry and his descendants with bell, book, and candle: whereupon he was dragged from the church and stoned to death. The story goes, however, that the last descendant of that particular branch of the Seymours was buried at Owslebury in a pauper's grave. The church itself seems to have been altered on several occasions in the 17th century. One guidebook describes it unkindly as having been "tinkered up by successive vicars with more zeal than artistic taste".

# Pamber

The church at Pamber has been described as "oddly French-looking", an indication perhaps of how completely Norman architecture has come to be considered indigenous to this country. It was built in 1110 by Henry de Port, son of the Hugh who did so well out of the Conquest (see Amport, Old Basing, Warnford, etc). Originally the Priory of West Sherborne—the ruins of the Benedictine monastery remain—it had a history which could politely be called chequered.

In 1446, a century before the Dissolution, Henry VI granted it to his new college at Eton. The prior and monks were expelled, the relics carried off, and prayers for the founder were dropped. In 1461 King Edward gave it to the Hospital of St Julian—"God's House"—at Southampton, which meant that in due course Queen's College was held responsible for the appointment and maintenance of "an honest priest". This duty it tried to evade on the grounds that the parish was legally responsible for upkeep of both church and priest. The parishioners, feeling otherwise, took the case to the Court of Chancery, and won.

The college then took an increasing interest in Pamber, even to the extent of removing in 1936 some unfortunate Victorian stained glass from the church and some 35 years later undertaking a programme of restoration and redecoration.

The surrounding woodland and heathland were once part of a royal hunting preserve (see Eversley), but the rights of chase were abandoned in 1605 after an official inquiry into the state of "Pambeare Forest" stated that "there hath been no deere in the same within memory of man".

The character of the countryside meant that the village maintained a tradition of such woodland crafts as rake-making well into this century. Mr Ernest Sims of Pamber End is, according to John Norden's *Craftsmen at Work*, probably the last man in southern England to be making the wooden rakes which were once in steady demand for the hayfields. There were even enough craftsmen to form a short-lived Rake and Sneadmakers' Union—Mr Sims, like other generations of his family during the past couple of centuries, used also to make scythe handles, or sneads.

# Penton Grafton 🦡

The ecclesiastical ups and downs—or rather ins and outs—which followed the Reformation were illustrated by the fortunes of the Sanctus Bell of the parish church. Struck in 1551, it disappeared after the reign of Catholic Mary and was found 20 years later sealed up in a niche; whereupon the rector—evidently of the Low Church persuasion—kept it on a desk in his study and used it to summon his servants. It was recovered, not without difficulty, from one of his descendants by a later rector, the Reverend William Badger, and returned to church use.

Religious intolerance of "dissenters" prompted the departure for the New World in 1638 of 13 emigrants from Penton Grafton including Peter Noyce or Noyes, yeoman. His servant John Rutter became the first carpenter in Sudbury, Massachusetts, where he built the Meeting House—there are still

Noyces and Rutters in the area. Noyes returned twice and took other settlers across the Atlantic with him. One was John Bent: his sister Ann died on the voyage but one of her sons, Samuel, may have been responsible for the naming of Andover, Mass., where he settled down.

They were a prolific family and by the War of Independence included farmers, blacksmiths, millers, bakers, and lawyers. One descendant, Silas, is reported to have been among those who threw the tea into Boston Harbour rather than pay British import tax on it. Others helped to open up the South West—Peter is believed to have survived a scalping by Red Indians.

# Popham 🖎

Lying halfway between London's Marble Arch and the Square at Portsmouth, the village was a staging point for coaches. The cottages later known as Popham Barracks provided food and refreshment for men and horses.

One Lord of the Manor was a Crusader; another provided a detachment of bowmen and spearmen for Agincourt—and helped to uncover the plot against Henry V, who tried the conspirators at Southampton, his port of embarkation, just before he set sail for France. The family's chapel by the old manor house—later Popham Court—was the original St Catherine's Church, which kept parish registers as far back as 1622.

In 1950 the *Hampshire Chronicle* recorded that after only 70 years the grey flint church which succeeded it fell down as a result of "heavy day and night traffic along the main road, the heavier military traffic preceding D-Day, blast from bombs and landmines, but above all to bad workmanship and poor material". And that was before they started building the motorway approaches!

Popham Beacon was a link in the chain of pre-telegraph invasion warnings. Driving south from London one still gets the slightly inaccurate feeling that from the high ground hereabouts it's downhill all the way.

# Portchester 🪶

Was it ever a village? The castle is famous, but it was always a military (or naval) strongpoint rather than a civilian settlement. The archaeologist Barry Cunliffe says that the fortifications—"a place of recreation, relaxation, and study"—lie in "the midst of an area of cluttered urban development".

The history of the place is therefore, until 20th-century housing spread along the shoreline, the history of its castle. The Roman fort was built not to subdue the British tribes but to help protect Roman Britain from Anglo-Saxon raiders. Possibly the builder was Carausius, a renegade Belgic-Roman admiral who declared UDI for Britannia. In about AD 370 the fort was abandoned in favour of Clausentum (Bitterne, Southampton) and there is then evidence of Saxon occupation—in fact those invaders had to re-fortify Portchester against Viking attacks later on. The Normans used it both as a royal residence and an embarkation point; it was strengthened during the Hundred Years War against the possibility of French raids, but with the onset of peace in 1399 was modernised by Richard II as a royal residence—though he was deposed before he could make much use of it.

The rise of Portsmouth led to Portchester's virtual abandonment, though it was used to house French prisoners during the Napoleonic Wars. If the situation elsewhere in Hampshire (see Bishop's Waltham, Hamble, and Odiham) is a guide it was at this period that the occupants of the castle had most to do with those who lived outside the walls. A proposal of 1855 that it should become a military hospital—see Netley Abbey—was mercifully rejected on the grounds that it was scarcely possible to choose a site less suitable.

Portchester (the place retains the "t" which Lord Porchester's family has somewhere abandoned), having spread along the shoreline, is still moving gradually up the slopes of Portsdown Hill. The motorway which now comes tearing down the chalk and out into the mudflats on the spur road to Portsea Island has done something to reduce the noise and congestion of the old coastal route between Southampton and Portsmouth.

138

Finally, the answer to the question with which I began. A print of the castle dated 1772 is captioned, inaccurately but entertainingly: "PORTCHESTER CASTLE takes its name from the village wherein it ftands .. It was once a town of note, then called Cäer-Peris. Stow, from Roufe, fays it was built by Gurgunftus, fon of Beline, who lived three hundred and feventy-feven years before Chrift; it was likewife, according to tradition, the place where Vefpafian landed: it had then a famous harbour; but the fea retiring, the inhabitants left the place and removed to the ifland of Portfey. . . . The caftle is a fquare whofe internal fide is four hundred and forty feet; its area contains four acres, four chains and feven perches. The walls are fix feet thick and about fifteen high, having in many places a paffage round them, covered with a parapet . . . On the infide, over the gate, are two projecting figures, fomewhat refembling Egyptian fphinxes".

How myfterious it all founds!

## Preston Candover (see The Candovers) 🙟

# Rockbourne 🙟

Hampshire County Council acquired in 1979 the site of the Roman villa, discovered in 1942 by a farmer trying to dig out a ferret, and identified as Roman by the amateur archaeologist he called in—Mr A. T. Morley Hewitt. An estate agent at Fordingbridge, it was he who also gave the parish the 4½-acre site of a pre-Roman encampment at Rockbourne Knoll.

Excavations at the villa produced a fine geometrical floor-mosaic with a swastika pattern as well as coins, imported Samian ware and New Forest pottery, and a *strigil* or scraper (predecessor of the loofah or bath-brush). With numerous rooms and underfloor central heating the villa was obviously the nucleus of an extensive farmstead.

The manor farm retains its 14th-century barn; nearby, the church—Norman in origin—seems to have lost its ghostly painting. A late Victorian guidebook reported "the occasional appearance of a medieval figure on the interior wall, caused perhaps by some ancient fresco showing its dim outline in damp weather beneath the modern [1892] whitewash".

The village, whose single street along a tiny stream-bed is described by Pevsner as "among the prettiest in Hampshire" was actually in Wiltshire until a revision of the county boundary in 1895.

The 100-foot tower on the high ground at West Park was erected in 1828 by the widow of General Sir Eyre Coote, who in the previous century had commanded the British troops in India.

# St Mary Bourne

The valley of what the Ordnance Survey calls the Bourne Rivulet (which is a bit like saying the Stream Stream) broadens out below the village just at the point where the London–Salisbury railway, following the line of the Test, needs to cross it. This provides two of the features which visitors most easily remember—the red-brick viaduct arching high above the rooftops and the wide watercress beds below.

A century ago the cress had its rivals in the way of village products. As elsewhere, basket-making flourished, but here the specialities were sieves for corn and the huckaback baskets used for barley in the process of brewing.

Staying away from the Bourne Revels might have been a useful tip for would-be octogenarians. These full-blooded July sports, which a century ago used to attract spectators from all the Bourne villages and contenders from Dorset and Somerset, included such events as cudgelling or backswording held on a platform built over the river. The backswordsman had his left arm tied to his side, leaving him defenceless against a wallop from the cudgel in his opponent's right. Scoring was by a crack on the skull, with extra marks if the blood ran down further than an inch. One expert saw the light, became a minister, and promptly denounced the games as scenes of "blood and drunkenness, sensuality and sin". No doubt many hot tempers were cooled when the backswordsmen fell off the platform into the stream.

140

Less brutal was "jingling", a variation on the theme of Blind Man's Bluff in which groups of men in blindfolds tried to catch a man who ran among them jingling handbells: the jingler who evaded capture might win a cheese or a barrel of beer, but the man who caught him could claim a purse of money.

A rare late-18th-century species of local enterprise in St Mary Bourne was oil-fuelled street-lighting, installed at the time of Queen Victoria's diamond jubilee. The silver jubilee of Queen Elizabeth was commemorated by the Women's Institute when a solitary surviving street-lamp—the rest had been melted down in a scrap-metal drive during the Second World War—was restored and wired for electricity.

It was the WI which recorded the decision of a former rector, the Reverend S. I. Lockhart, to have a coffin built for him in his lifetime by the village carpenter, Mr Batsford, out of wood from a tree in the rectory garden. He tried it for size several times to make sure it was big enough, and when he eventually died he left instructions that his books were to be buried with him. Unfortunately there were so many that the lid couldn't be screwed down! He was survived by the carpenter—long remembered as an old man with a long white beard who walked about the village with a pet goose that hissed at strangers.

His sister Fanny lived to the age of 103, one of several centenarians whose longevity was taken as proof of the local saying that in St Mary Bourne you may live as long as you please.

Gilbert White Museum, Selborne.

# Selborne

*The Natural History of Selborne*, the Reverend Gilbert White's perennial best-seller, brings visitors in their thousands to the village. It remains unspoiled, partly, perhaps, because most of the visitors are instinctively discreet in observing even the human fauna they identify, and partly because the denizens of this particular Hampshire habitat remain natural.

The village is in my experience unique in having two pubs both of which provide good beer, good food, and a good welcome. One December I was startled while ordering a pint in the Selborne Arms by a loud crash and a cry of "Oh, KNICKERS!", but it was only a minor mishap with the Christmas decorations, and the pot-au-feu—literally, a cast-iron cauldron of stew hooked on to the bars of a vast log fire in the bar—was as well under control as ever.

This is farming country, much admired for its soil by Cobbett. It was a farmer who gave his name to White's home, Wakes (somehow "The" has crept in), in the village street. It remained a private house until 1953 but is now a museum and study centre. A good deal of Selborne remains—as does Wakes and its garden—as the parson-naturalist described it. This includes the "hollow lanes, by the traffic of ages and the fretting of the water worn down in many places 16 or 18 feet

142

below the level of the fields"—though his comment that "these rugged gloomy scenes affright the ladies" may be less valid than it was in 1768.

Nore Hill above the village is the source of two streams which join different seaboards. One joins (via the Wey) the Thames and flows into "the German Ocean"; the other "becomes a branch of the Arun, running to Arundel and so falling into the British Channel".

Selborne was one of the villages most affected by the agricultural riots of the 1830s. In their classic work *The Village Labourer*, J. L. and Barbara Hammond paint a picture of local farmworkers confronting the Reverend William Cobbold with the words: "We must have a touch of your tithes: we think £300 a year is quite enough for you." Mr Cobbold's income from tithes was then twice that amount (my own father's total stipend in a parish 15 miles away a century later was £342). The "Selborne Mob" included a number of farmers who promised their workers higher wages if their tithe payments were reduced. The demonstrators won a temporary victory and went on to burn down the local workhouse, a few miles away at Headley, sparing only a ward in which sick paupers were lying. Mr Cobbold belatedly bought himself a mastiff for protection against further "persuasion" and equipped it with a heavy collar, which was subsequently hung up in the church—possibly to give the congregation something to think about as well as the sermon.

Many different editions of White's *Natural History* and his other writings are to be found on the shelves of the bookshop next to his old home. Mrs Anne Mallinson has specialised since 1968 in books dealing with every conceivable aspect of life in the country, with due prominence given not only to Parson White but also Jane Austen (see Chawton), Edward Thomas (see Steep) and Flora Thompson (see Grayshott). There is also a National Trust corner with various publications illustrating the NT's interests and activities, and showing the areas it owns in Selborne. These include, as well as the common with the famous hanger and hill, some strips on the other side of the village street including the Lythe or Lyth (it rhymes with myth).

The poet Anthony Rye, who lived in a house on high ground overlooking this delightful miniature valley, led the opposition to a scheme to use it for sewerage. As a reporter I was once instructed to seek his views on the subject (they contrasted with those of villagers fed up with having to use privies at the end of the garden).

Years later after a chance second meeting in the Queen's Arms he gave me a copy of his collection *The Inn of the Birds* . . . was this gentle pastoral poet the last of the Neo-Georgians? I remember from our conversation the particular delight he took in Gilbert White's discovery, with the aid of a friend who possessed a pitch-pipe, that owls hoot in B flat.

# Soberton

It's not that the other end of the original parish, Meonstoke, was particularly drunken. This was the Sudbertune, or South Barton—barton being usually an outlying farm. Oddly, although it wasn't made a separate parish until 1897, it had a complete parochial organisation of its own and the list of incumbents goes back to 1282. Victorian restoration of the church included work on the tower. The carving of a key and a bucket records that butlers and other house-servants contributed £70 to the work in 1880.

This is the parish where downland chalk meets ancient woodland. Pub names past and present are links with the forest of Bere: the Buck's Head, the Falcon, the Forester, the Green Man, and the Roebuck. As a hunting preserve its history goes back to the Saxon Earl Godwin, father of King Harold, who held two manors in Soberton.

The village provided a modest home in Cromwellian times for Walter Curle (see Bishop's Waltham). His sister offered him a refuge after his escape from Waltham in a manure cart during the Roundheads' attack on the episcopal palace. In fact Cromwell caught up with him in the siege of Winchester but was content to strip him of his riches and let him go. He died in 1647 and is buried in what became the Curle chapel in the parish church.

A gravestone of 1783 begs passers-by to "shed a bitter tear" for a sailor murdered on the road to Hambledon. Better fortune attended Baron Soberton, who as Commodore Anson returned to Portsmouth in 1744 after a round-the-world expedition which included harassing Spanish treasure-ships in the Pacific. He brought back the biggest prize of bullion ever captured. His last command before retiring to the Meon Valley (and thereby setting something of a precedent for naval officers) was in 1747, when he destroyed the French fleet off Finistère.

# Sparsholt 🪶

A rudimentary health service which was operated by the parish overseer in the first quarter of the last century demonstrates that even then there was a demand for sleeping pills. One set of accounts shows that 2s 6d was spent on them, while other items were The Mixture, 3s; and Lotion, 5s 6d. One lad was given an emetic, a blister, and a draught (total bill: 3s) on one day, a pint of The Mixture on the next, and further treatment (including three leeches) later the same week.

He might have preferred a drop of contraband whisky such as caused the court appearance in 1828 of four Sparsholt men. They were fined sums between £12 10s and £25—two of them for the unlawful possession of spirits, two for selling them. The contraband came up from the coast and was dropped in Hursley if the Revenue Men were spotted—and probably if they were not, since according to a report in the *Hampshire Chronicle*, "the extent of these illegal practices attracted the attention of the Minister, and the Excise Officers were put in possession of the evidence".

In the non-alcoholic sense, however, Sparsholt was high and dry, with its share of farm fires. Sixteen horses and a wide range of agricultural implements were lost at Westley in 1872. The farmer's son galloped to Winchester for help and the 46th Regiment obligingly sent a squad of firefighters and a fire-engine, both of which proved useless in the absence of a water-supply: indeed, the soldiers demanded that the distraught farmer's wife should provide them with a meal. On top of that a crowd of sightseers from Winchester arrived as if for a barbecue, and helped themselves to roast chicken and pork at the farmer's expense.

In dry summers even drinking water had to be carted up from Winchester, the only village supply being a 247-foot well topped by a shed in which was a treadmill: it took two men 20 minutes to draw up the bucket. In 1897, however, the diamond jubilee of Queen Victoria was marked by the erection of a brick and tile building with a storage tank and a mechanical pump, originally operated by a windmill. When Sparsholt's first constable was appointed his duties included the apprehension of "mischievous village boys damaging the well". I wonder what his attitude was to the device rigged up by one villager which, so the story goes, drew him a bucket of water every time anyone opened his garden gate?

In those days, a century or so ago, the village still had a Waywarden (see Beaulieu). He kept the parish roads in repair with the help of such inhabitants as Mrs Nellie Kirby, who even in old age would put on a clean white apron every day and go out into the fields to gather flints which she would put in piles on the verges for roadmending.

The landlord of the Woodman Inn at Sparsholt, John Baigent Lewington, was also coachman to the Assize Court Judge at Winchester: he last drove the coach during the First World War. He also possessed a brougham, which for many years provided a home for one Jake Avery. Kept later in a barn at Moor Court Farm, it ended its days by being dragged into a pond and set on fire.

In 1926 the main building of the County Farm Institute, now the Hampshire College of Agriculture, was built: in 1978 its dormitories were replaced by four halls of residence containing 64 study-bedrooms. This expansion reflected the growth both in scope and stature of the college, which trebled in size during the seventies.

# Steep 🌿

Most of the village is at the bottom of the wooded escarpment, overlooked by the sarsen stone on Shoulder of Mutton Hill which is a simple memorial to the poet Edward Thomas. He lived at Berryfield Cottage at the beginning of the century, moved to Week Green on the hilltop, and then down again to Yew Tree Cottage which was his home from 1913–16. Killed at the Battle of Arras in the following year he is commemorated in the parish church by a memorial window designed by Laurence Whistler. It was dedicated in 1978, the centenary of his birth, by the parson-poet, R. S. Thomas. Edward's first published poem, "Up in the Wind", contains a reference to an isolated pub on the plateau above the village. It is the White Horse, where he is remembered by a modest plaque naming one of two hospitable rooms The Edward Thomas Bar.

The Thomas children went to school at Bedales, almost opposite their home. Founded in Sussex in 1893, its aim was to modify, not repudiate, the English public school system. It came to Steep a few years later and admitted girls, not to challenge convention but because its founder, John Haden Badley, was "always ready to adopt any idea which fitted in with his general principles". James L. Henderson, a member of the staff from 1934–40, recalled in his book about the school (*Irregularly Bold*: Deutsch, 1978) that: "It cannot be emphasised too often just how bold and unconventional—indeed, outrageous—in the eyes of some, particularly some of the Hampshire county folk, the whole Bedalian venture was".

But in contrast to such local lay opinions as "enthusiastic amateurs dealing with children of cranks", official reports from the Board of Education included "an interesting, if not unique, educational experiment" (1902) and "While it does some things that very few other schools attempt, it does thoroughly well what other good schools do" (1909).

Dr Henderson thinks it is a gigantic—and unresolved—paradox that the school started out as an "innovatory pioneering movement in a basically self-confident late-Victorian society and became an assured, successful, and established institution in a society which has been increasingly fragmented".

# Steventon 🦢

Little but a memorial in the parish church—and a pump in a field near by where the rectory stood—remains to connect the village with Jane Austen (see Chawton). But she was born in the rectory in 1775—it was demolished about a century later—and it was her home until 1801. And it was at Steventon that she worked on *Sense and Sensibility*, *Pride and Prejudice*, and *Northanger Abbey*. Her father, it is recorded, kept five Alderneys—at a time when the notion of special dairy cows was considered something of an innovation. Not only Jane and her family benefited but also those children which her father, like many other country parsons of his time, taught in a room at his own home.

His parishioners, too, operated their cottage industries. Both flax and wool were spun in the village in the 18th century. Many of these modest homes outlasted the Manor House, which was occupied by the Services during the war, left empty, and wrecked by vandals.

# Stockbridge 🦢

The Test is shallow and divided here, and its valley wide enough to have provided a river crossing since earliest times, and a posting station in Roman times on the road from Winchester to Sarum. The bridges came later: a plaque on one besought passers-by

"Say of your cheryte a paternoster and an ave for the sowlyss of John Gylmyn otherwise seyde Lokke and Richard Gater and Margrete the wyf of the forsayd John and Richard founderys and makerys of ye sayd bryge yn whos sowlys God have mercy".

Their bridge was replaced in 1792: the latest dates from 1962. As to the "stock"—the biggest herds to cross the Test here were Welsh cattle being driven to the great fairs and markets of Surrey and Kent. These journeys across the width of England ended with the coming of the railways, and you can still see a notice painted on a former inn at Stockbridge (now a private house) advertising "Gwair Tymherus, Porfa Flasus, Cwrw Da, a Cwal Cysurus"—Worthwhile Grass, Pleasant Pasture, Good Beer and Comfortable Shelter.

This is farming and racing country. In 1632 a plough was demonstrated at Stockbridge "that by the help of engines and some contrivances might be drawn by dogs and managed by one man, and would plough in one day well-nigh an acre of light ground".

Two houses are named after Derby successes. The Cossacks, originally a pub named after the 1847 winner, and Hermit Lodge (Hermit won in a snowstorm at 100–1 in 1877). Pictured in a roundel over the door leading to the choir vestry in St Peter's Church is The Tetrarch, trained by Atty Persse at Chattis Hill Stables. Ridden in all his races by Steve Donoghue, who then lived at Winton House, Stockbridge, Tetrarch was never beaten. Foaled in 1911, he was sold the following year for 1,300 guineas.

The original St Peter's fell into disuse with the building of the new church in 1866, but was rehallowed in 1963: it is used as a mortuary chapel, and for an annual service.

An observation on the spiritual well-being of the parish was made when a Cistercian monk who could see devils found only one at Stockbridge Fair but dozens in the priory at Mottisfont. When he caught one and asked it about this discrepancy, it replied that souls were easy to come by at Stockbridge, but at Mottisfont it needed concentrated effort to provoke even the smallest sin.

The title to the manorial rights was discovered in the 'twenties as an unredeemed pledge left with a London pawnbroker. Sir Norman Hill, who acquired both title and manor, set about reviving the ancient Courts Leet and Baron. After his death the Lordship was bequeathed to the National Trust and operated on their behalf by his daughter Rosalind, who has presided knowledgeably and energetically over the discussion of such problems as harrowing the marsh, keeping the services of a district nurse, fishing rights, rabbit catching, ale-testing, and the obstruction of downland by wire fencing.

From 1562–1832 the 70 voters on the electoral roll returned two Members to Parliament. In 1680 a vote could be bought

149

for about five guineas but inflation set in and by 1790 the going rate was about 70 guineas. In 1831 the honour of representing the rottenest of boroughs cost a candidate £1,000 a seat. There are several versions of what happened to Richard Steele, of *The Spectator*, when he sought re-election. One says simply that he was told he would not be chosen unless he presented an apple stuffed with guineas to an important elector's wife; another that he was not re-elected because he never fulfilled a promise to present an apple stuffed with guineas to the couple who should first produce a child nine months after his election.

The electoral malpractices even attracted a barb from John Gay, satirist of *The Beggars' Opera*:

> Sutton we pass, and leave her spacious down,
> And with the setting sun reach Stockbridge town;
> O'er our parched tongue the rich metheglin glides
> And the red dainty trout our knife divides.
> Sad melancholy ev'ry visage wears:
> What, no election come in seven long years?

More verse was composed in memory of John Buckett, landlord of the King's Head, who died in 1802:

> And is alas! Poor Buckett gone?
> Farewell, convivial honest John.
> Oft at the well, by fatal stroke,
> Buckets—like pitchers—must be broke:
> In this same motley, shifting scene
> How various have thy fortunes been!
> Now lifted high, now sinking low,
> Today thy brim would overflow—
> Thy bounty then would all apply
> To fill and drink, and leave thee dry;
> Tomorrow sunk as in a well
> Content, unseen, with truth to dwell.
> But high or low, or wet or dry,
> No rotten stave could malice spy:
> Then rise, immortal Buckett, rise
> And claim thy station in the skies—
> 'Twixt Amphora and Pisces shine,
> Still guarding Stockbridge with thy sign.

# Sway 🌿

It must have seemed to villagers that Judge Andrew Peterson was tempting providence when a century ago he built a 218-foot high tower in concrete—then a largely experimental material—in a place with the name of Sway.

Perhaps it was his contention (he was a Spiritualist) that the design had been given to him by Sir Christopher Wren, through a medium, that most upset those whose property lay in the shadow of what has been called Peterson's Folly—a nickname which has upset at least one descendant of the workmen who built it. "Both my parents worked for Peterson", wrote Mr Gilbert Chase of Milford-on-Sea in 1979, "and they have told me a different story. Personally I think it was built with the very good intention of helping working people in and around Sway."

This was certainly the result, but Peterson seems to have been a far-sighted man who predicted a great future for Portland cement concrete—reinforced with metal rods—and, at Sway, pioneered the "shutter" method of construction, an adaptation perhaps of the method of building mud walls which he had seen on his travels in India—he was a member of the Calcutta Bar and deputised as a High Court Judge. It dispensed with the need for elaborate scaffolding: concrete was set in wooden frames and the height built up a few feet at a time.

Peterson had settled at Sway in 1868 when he retired, and he built a smaller concrete tower by way of a prototype in the grounds of his house, now known as Arnewood Towers. The "folly" was completed in the 1880s. It has 13 storeys, but the builders' luck—and their concrete—held and the structure, somewhere in style between Italianate and Victorian Gothic, is still a famous New Forest landmark. The judge's ashes, interred in a vault below the tower upon his death in 1906 at the age of 93, were re-interred in his wife's grave in Sway churchyard at the request of relatives when the tower was sold in 1957. It now belongs to Mr Paul Atlas, who bought it "simply because it was at the bottom of his garden". Though strengthened (and equipped with a lightning conductor) it is out of bounds to the public.

The growth of Bournemouth put an end to the expansion of Sway. This was nothing deliberate—merely the result of re-routing the railway line between Southampton and Dorchester (see Brockenhurst). "Castleman's Corkscrew", as it was called, wriggled across the forest by way of Sway, Ringwood, and Wimborne. It was only at the turn of the century, some 50 years later, that the London and South Western found that there were sufficient inhabitants and holiday-makers at Bournemouth to justify a line to what had been a cluster of fisherman's huts at the mouth of a wooded chine. The old route was abandoned altogether before Sway could become anything like the commuter centre of Brockenhurst, the next station up the line to Southampton and London.

Many journalists collect newspaper headlines, which is at worst a fairly harmless form of masochism and at best a continual source of hilarity. One of my favourites is an item of ecclesiastical intelligence which emphasised the advisability of building on rocks, as advocated in the Gospel according to St Matthew, Chapter XVI, verse 18. The arrival of a new incumbent was headed "Bursledon Vicar Going To Sway". Whoops!

# Tadley

Like many villages on the Hampshire–Berkshire border Tadley—despite growing suburbanisation—maintains its centuries-old tradition of craftsmanship based on the surrounding woodland. J. Geraint Jenkins records in *Traditional Craftsmen*, published in 1979, that broomsquires were still turning out the traditional birch besoms—but that the number had diminished rapidly with the establishment at Aldermaston of the Atomic Weapons Research Establishment. It not only attracted labour but was sited on the sandy heathland which had provided the craft with its raw materials. Mr Alfred West is quoted as probably the last of a long line of broomsquires— "he uses exactly the same techniques of manufacture and the few simple tools that his ancestor used when, 400 years ago, he established his business on the brow of Mulford's Hill".

Village crafts and trades were depicted on the Tadley Roll, a kind of Victorian strip cartoon amateurishly but vividly drawn on a three-inch-wide strip of paper and showing the entire population in the late 1870s. Not only local families were depicted but also a visiting party of map-makers from the Royal Engineers (perhaps one of them was the artist). Possibly it was the resultant map of north Hampshire which helped to persuade the ecclesiastical authorities that Tadley deserved to be a parish on its own; until 1978 it was a chapelry of Overton, eight miles away to the south-west even for a fit crow with a good sense of direction.

This is more than can be said of the pioneer balloonist who inadvertently landed at Tadley and asked where he was. A startled villager observing his descent from above replied "Tadley, God save us!" and Tadley Godsaveus it became.

# Thruxton ✤

To the motor racing enthusiast Thruxton means the circuit built on the old airfield. To 19th-century wayfarers it meant a tollgate on the Amesbury Turnpike (to the compilers of the Domesday Book it meant a manor held by Gozelin de Cormelies). The tollkeeper's cottage was sold by the turnpike company in 1871 to a local innkeeper, John Emm, for £60. In 1965, by which time it was a café, it was bulldozed in the course of a road-widening scheme.

Thruxton, like many another village, acquired a church school in Victorian times. In 1966, when it closed after 100 years, memories of early days were still sharp. Miss Elsie Nixon, then aged 83, recalled going to school in 1887. The headmaster she described as tall, well-built, very strict and often impatient. This was more than a schoolchild's view—the head she pictured so objectively was her own father, Edwin, who held the post for 37 years and died in 1928; both his son and grandson became teachers.

Catholic Chapel
Tichborne Park

R.C.G

# Tichborne 🦢

Deserving local ladies continue to receive bags of flour in a revival of the Tichborne Dole, which originated in the reign of Henry I. Sir Roger Tichborne's dying and bedridden wife asked if he would give some land to endow a charitable trust, and the cunning man promised as much as she could drag herself round while a firebrand stayed alight. The lady then managed to crawl around twenty odd acres, and the field near the village is still called The Crawls. She then made sure her husband kept his promise by laying a curse on the family if the produce from the land ever ceased to be distributed anually. It has been ever since—more or less without a break. Nearly 2,000 loaves used to be distributed but in 1894, because of "unseemly scenes" money was handed out instead. During the Second World War news leaked out that the Ministry of Food had granted Sir Anthony Doughty-Tichborne's request for extra coupons—both bread and flour were rationed—to keep the tradition going in something like its old form. The Ministry panicked and withdrew its offer, whereupon Sir Anthony wrote to *The Times* and bread coupons came in from all over the country.

The name of family and village is derived from At Itchenbourne; the source of the stream is nearby (see Cheriton) and flows through the park. Chidiock Tichborne, beheaded for his involvement in a conspiracy on behalf of Mary Queen of Scots, claimed the family had been there two centuries before the Norman Conquest. They remained staunchly Roman Catholic and somehow the family chapel in the parish church survived Reformation, Puritanism, and all kinds of ecclesiastical upheaval.

Their name became world-famous, and their finances dwindled, in Victorian times when the heir—another Sir Roger—disappeared in Australia. The man who returned to claim the inheritance was pronounced, after a protracted trial which put £80,000 into the pockets of the legal profession, a butcher from London named Arthur Orton. The imposter (if such he was: many remained unconvinced) was jailed for 14 years but the Tichborne fortunes never really recovered. When Sir Anthony died in 1968 he left £211, having avoided death duties by selling his life interest in the estate to his three daughters.

In 1902 Mrs Emily Park took over the thatched post-office. She was then 54. She was still postmistress in her 94th year, 1942, when the village took part in a summer savings campaign, War Weapons Week. Achieving its target of £50 enabled Tichborne to buy the army a bren gun.

# Tidworth 🦢

Thomas Assheton Smith, a wealthy man born in 1776, built Tedworth House in 1830 on the Hampshire–Wiltshire borders. The old spelling is preserved in the Tedworth Hunt, of which he was Master for 50 years—hunting until he was 80 and becoming a living legend in the process. "The most courageous fox-hunter in England" was one verdict. "Tom Smith" formed his own company of yeomanry, which was duly inspected—and praised—by the Duke of Wellington.

It was a later owner of Tedworth House, Sir John Kelk, who sold out to the Army altogether at the turn of the century; the building became administrative headquarters for the Salisbury Plain area, and was used later as an officers' club.

In 1919 the author of *Highways and Byways of Hampshire* wrote: "It will not be long before impressionist paragraphist and ill-informed sightseer may be bemoaning here the ruin wrought in the beautiful county by that Aunt Sally for experimenting politicians and armchair critics, the poor little British Army! As for the Tedworth Downs—well, come and see them in their nakedness while Tedworth Camp is yet in its initial stage of unredeemed ugliness, whilst everything is so new that the 'spoiling process' may be marked from its inception. The tin-hutted camp is as ugly as a camp can manage to be; this quiet little village, the 'model village' as the sporting writer Nimrod had called Tom Smith's Tedworth, is no more".

And, though I was brought up midway between Bordon and Aldershot, I was still startled on a visit to Tidworth five or six years ago to see what is considered good enough for soldiers and their families in the way of new quarters purpose-built three-quarters of the way through the 20th century.

The Army did, however, bring the railway to the village—or rather to the camp: they paid for it, and it was ready for summer manoeuvres in 1901. It was open to public passenger traffic from 1902–55. Terminus of the only branch line on the Midland and South Western Junction Railway, it had the highest receipts of any station on the entire system and was used in the days of the Tidworth Tattoo to bring passengers in special trains from all over the country. A good deal of manoeuvring had gone on to get the railway built at all. As one of a number of grandiose schemes to connect the Midlands (and hence Wales and the North) with the South Coast, the Midland and South Western Junction Railway began running through trains from Southampton to Cheltenham in 1892.

At the end of the Boer War the Undersecretary for War thanked the company for carrying men, horses, and stores bound for South Africa. He may have felt privately it was the least it could have done, since it was the War Department which had paid £4,000 for the platform, bay line, and engine-shed at Ludgershall, where the branch to Tidworth left the main line.

The name of Tedworth/Tidworth had become famous all over the country in the 17th century as a result of what now seems a classic poltergeist case, though the usual explanation of the time was witchcraft. In 1662 John Mompesson of North Tedworth, a Justice of the Peace, confiscated the drum of William Drury, a beggar, who was using the drum to draw attention to his plight. This was accepted practice for old soldiers, but Mompesson believed his papers were forged. The drum was taken to Mompesson's house, and very soon the family was kept awake by thumping and drumming— Mompesson identified one theme as the tune "Roundheads and Cuckolds goe digge, goe digge".

Later the children's bedsteads and mattresses were scrabbled at and pushed about, and household articles thrown all over the place. Mompesson burned the drum but the disturbances continued and were experienced not only by the family and servants but by visitors. ("Some have had their hands catched as they have been feeling for a chamber pot and their feet and stomachs layed on"). Blue lights were seen to shine and glimmer.

As with other similar manifestations, there was a little girl in the household—two, in fact: but the phenomena ceased at about the time when Drury, who had been sentenced to transportation for stealing pigs, escaped from custody in the Bristol Channel, returned to Wiltshire, and was re-arrested. Charged this time with witchcraft, he was acquitted.

I have, by the way, cheated by including this story. North Tidworth is in Wiltshire. The county boundary is, however, so little in evidence that even the railway station was built right across it.

# Titchfield 🎵

Like Hamble, Titchfield was at the same time a village and a port: but it grew faster and then lost its seaward link when the first Earl of Southampton had the River Meon dammed by Dutch engineers to prevent flooding. Some say that the burning of his effigy was the origin of the annual carnival now grafted on to the village's Bonfire Day celebrations. The Earl was of course Thomas Wriothesley, Chancellor to Henry VIII. Engineering the Dissolution of the Monasteries gave him first pick of properties newly on the market and available for development. He pulled down Titchfield's 13th-century abbey and built himself Place House—demolished in its turn, except for the old gatehouse, by later owners who used the stone to extend their own home near Fareham, Cams Hall.

It was the third Earl who was Shakespeare's host, patron, admirer, and possibly something more. Some of the sonnets are said to have been written at Titchfield and claims have been made that Place House was the scene of world premières for "Love's Labour's Lost", "Romeo and Juliet", "Midsummer Night's Dream", and "Twelfth Night". The Wriothesley monument is in the south chapel of the parish church, where the porch of an 8th- or 9th-century church has been incorporated into the base of the tower.

The short road to the church is older in appearance than the wide square from which it leads, but this is largely because its houses did not receive so much "modernisation" in Georgian times. The process meant that elegant regular façades were imposed on a number of much earlier buildings—and also that the market hall, complete with lock-up jail in one corner, was shunted round the corner out of sight and allowed to decay to the point where the local authorities—Hampshire County Council and Fareham Urban Council—were in 1971 prepared to allow it to be demolished. Luckily local indignation, with the help of individuals and organisations interested in preserving the past, generated sufficient funds and enthusiasm to

158

enable the building to be dismantled piece by piece and re-erected in the Weald and Downland Open Air Museum at Singleton in West Sussex.

While the process was still going on I asked the director how much guesswork was going into restoring the 17th-century hall to its original appearance. A certain amount of conjecture, he said, was inevitable, but they had other examples to go on and the craftsmen working on the project knew, for instance, where to fit new timber since the original frame still had the mortices into which the replacements were being slotted.

The spirit which saved the market hall (though, alas, no place could be found for it in Titchfield) has been partly responsible for keeping the feel, and to some extent the appearance, of a village. It was the first entire parish to be designated a conservation area under the Civic Amenities Act. How much that would have meant had the ghastly notion of a Solent City linking Portsmouth and Southampton ever materialised is a matter of horrifying guesswork.

# Totton 🌿

In 1855 Totton, then "the principal hamlet in the parish of Eling", was notable for "50 acres of excellent saltmarsh over which the inhabitants enjoy a common run for feed of cattle from Hawk Monday till the longest day, when only seven persons are privileged to turn in one horse to feed over the whole". The common marsh was then closed for a month to allow it to recover.

The name Totton is said to mean "the settlement of Tota's people"—in the Domesday Book, Totintone. Scorn was poured on a recent suggestion that it was "To town"—that is, from an Eling point of view, on the way to Southampton. On the other hand, somebody once asked a Greek bound for Constantinople where he was going, and he replied "To the town": only, being Greek, he said Eis ten polin, which became in Turkish Istambul or Stamboul. . . .

A genuine Turkish connection was provided by Colonel Edward Birch Reynardson who commanded the Grenadier Guards at Inkerman and Sebastopol. On returning home to

Rushington Manor he buried his cloak under a stone bearing the words.

> Beneath this spot lies buried here
> The coat I wore in the Crimea.
> In former days it served me well
> As Alma and Inkerman both can tell.
> Farewell, ye relics of the fight—
> In memory still, though lost to sight.

The stone—but not the cloak!—was moved when Testbourne House was built in the thirties on the site of the manor.

By 1870 Totton had its own brewery—Ashby's in Rumbridge Street—and two blacksmiths: one was a woman, Martha Maynard. The old tollhouse on the Salisbury turnpike operated as a flour mill for 40 years from 1895. A famous tradesman of the turn of the century was Mr C. F. Batt, who bought two cottages at what is now Batt's Corner and put up a shop which sold "almost everything except food". He died in 1901 but the business was carried on, first by his wife and then by his daughters, until 1952.

Thirty years ago a Scotsman who had settled in the neighbourhood told me he believed the dramatic increase in the population of Totton was due to the fact that a train passed through at 5.30 every morning, which was "too late to go to sleep again and too early to get dressed"! For the truth about the "largest village" controversy, turn back to the parent parish of Eling.

# Twyford ❧

The existence of sarsen stones near this settlement at the place of Two Fords over the Itchen is a matter of geological record, not a relic of Druidical enthusiasm. When Winchester was Venta Belgarum there was a Roman farmstead or villa here: it was discovered in 1891.

A Roman Catholic school originating at Silkstead, near Hursley, moved to an Elizabethan farmhouse known as Segar's House or Seagar's Buildings at Twyford. The last Segar had died in 1690, leaving a chalice and patten to the parish church. Eight-year-old Alexander Pope became a pupil in 1697 but was expelled for writing some satirical verses about his tutor. It was suggested in this century that the building might make a headquarters for Hampshire Field Club, but 20 years ago it was pulled down to make way for a housing estate.

The present Twyford School is one of the oldest preparatory schools in the country. Its condition in 1830 is described, not very flatteringly, by an early pupil—Thomas Hughes—in *Tom Brown's Schooldays*.

Benjamin Franklin's autobiography is dated "Twyford, at the Bishop of St Asaph's, 1771". The Bishop was Jonathan Shipley, a sympathiser with the movement for American independence, whose home was at Twyford House.

It was also in the 18th century that William Davies lost his way when riding home in a thick October fog. He took his bearings from the sound of the bells of Twyford Church—avoiding a deep chalkpit just in time. In gratitude he left "to the ringers of the parish of Twyford the sum of 20 shillings to be paid them every year for ever on the 7th of October provided that they ring on the morning and evening of that day, but not otherwise". The custom was abandoned during the Second World War, when church bells would have meant a German invasion, but revived later.

Another noisy celebration which died out altogether was the anvil-banging with which the blacksmiths, harmonious or otherwise, celebrated their annual holiday on the feast of St Clement.

# Upham

Evidence of a local craft survives in a pub name, the Brush-maker's Arms. 20 years ago there was a good deal of rivalry between the regulars and those of the Jubilee Tavern in the neighbouring hamlet of Dundridge. The latter, now poshed up and renamed, was in my young days a pretty basic establishment. Its patrons, numerous, enthusiastic and drawn from a wide area, were in effect a kind of supporters' club and one evening I was sworn to secrecy about a plot to construct an outsize besom and "show the flag" by ramming it down the chimney of the Brushmaker's.

Such frivolity would have been frowned on by the 18th-century poet Edward Young, author of a gloomy—but, in his own day, popular—collection of verses entitled "Night Thoughts". Sample: "Night, sable goddess! from her ebon throne/In rayless majesty, now stretches forth/Her leaden sceptre o'er a slumb'ring world." Leaden is the word, though he was also responsible for the epitaph on Voltaire, "You are so witty, profligate and thin/At once we think thee Milton, Death, and sin." But it was Edward Young, whose father was rector of Upham and a royal chaplain, who first remarked "Procrastination is the thief of time".

Stories about Cromwell's troops using churches to stable their horses are legion. At Upham an entry in the registers notes the cost of cleaning out the chancel after their occupation by the Roundhead cavalry.

# Upton Grey 🍂

Three crosses cut in the west wall of the (basically Norman) church are said to indicate where the bishop who consecrated the building laid his hands during the ceremony. Extensions and renovations continued over five centuries and an unusual feature is an external staircase leading to the belfry.

The church overlooks cottages clustered round a village pond which also had an episcopal connection in recent years. An article in the *Southern Evening Echo* recorded that a resident duck and drake, Jemima and Butch, produced a duckling whose neck feathers bore white markings which gave him a pronouncedly ecclesiastical look. He was promptly named Faulkner, after Dr Faulkner Allison, Bishop of Winchester.

When it was decided to commemorate Winston Churchill by planting trees in Upton Grey much thought was given to choosing suitable species. Oak now commemorates his qualities as a statesman, and maple is a reminder of his North American blood.

162

# Vernham Dean 🕮

The distance between church and village in this scattered settlement, one of several among the fields and woodlands sloping up towards the border with Wiltshire and Berkshire, reflects a story dating from the days of the Plague.

The legend is that the rector persuaded his parishioners to gather in a spot well away from the village while he went to Andover for food supplies and medical help. He left them, intending to escape, but was then himself struck down by the infection while still on Vernham Hill.

His ghost is said to haunt the area still: in 1949 a woman cycling home to Fosbury reported seeing a figure "white from the waist upwards, wearing a robe which swung from the movement of his legs", but as she approached the figure disappeared among the trees at the side of the road.

# The Wallops 🕮

In Old English "waella" means stream and "hop" means valley, so we shall have to forget other more entertaining derivations for Wollop Inferior or Nether Wallop, Wollop Superior or Over Wallop, and other variations on the names of the settlements along the valley of the little stream.

The manor of Over Wallop was held by Godiva, wife of Leofric of Mercia: she may even have been born here. After her time it seems to have escaped most of the vexations of history until 1787, when 2,000 acres of common land were enclosed. The same thing happened ten years later at Nether Wallop. Here outbreaks of fire used to cause devastation at intervals. In 1672 "the Great Fire caused losses of £8,000 and upwards"; in 1739, 18 dwelling-houses together with barns, stables and other out-houses were burned down; the following century there was a fire at the Manor Farm, and when helpers were offered a pint of beer for their efforts, 210 persons came forward. The manor was rebuilt in 1934 after another out-break during which the butler was observed pouring water on the flames from a jug.

An earlier conflagration was dealt with more efficiently—in 1887 an old man threw what he thought was a dead match on to the thatched roof of a privy, and the flames spread to a woman's straw hat, but no further damage seems to have occurred.

In 1928, thatched cottages in Bolton's Row were struck by lightning and destroyed by fire, but flames were prevented spreading further by the combined efforts of the local cricket team and their opponents from RAMC Tidworth.

Incidentally, some of the first cricket-bats are said to have been made from willows growing in the Wallop Brook. A later crop was watercress.

An 18th-century Doctor of Physic, Francis Douce, built a pyramid memorial in the churchyard at Nether Wallop. He also left £1,000 invested for boys and girls of the parish to be "taught to read and write and cast an account a little way, especially those who cannot pass for schooling and learning; but they must not go too far lest it makes them saucy and all the girls want to be chambermaids and in a few years you will be in want of cooks". His pyramid had to be kept in good order, "and if the Parish boys do climb or injure it they shall not only be deprived of their learning but also be punished". By the 20th century his charity was being used to help local children with uniforms and textbooks.

# Warnford

The biggest non-ecclesiastical landowner in the Domesday Book, Hugh de Port, held Warnford Manor. Its Saxon Lord had been Alward, but it looks as though the family enjoyed remarkable staying power since Peake Farm was the birthplace of James Aylward—still a Meon Valley name—who scored 167 runs in the famous match when Hambledon made 403 and beat All England, "batting from 5 o'clock on Wednesday until 3 o'clock on Friday".

Hugh's great-grandson Adam "restored" the Saxon church in the 13th century and built St John's House. It was in ruins by the 17th century, but was roofed in and used as a barn. A century later the roof was taken off again so that the remains could form a picturesque ruin in the grounds of a new house built for William Neale. A lifelong gambler who became Master of the Mint, he organised our first State Lottery.

In the 18th century the estate reverted, after a fashion, to the Normans—the Neales sold it to the de Burghs, Earls of Clanricarde. The family had, according to a newspaper account, "sought refuge in England after they had been driven out of Ireland by revolting peasants". After a brief period in which the Clanricardes called the estate Sanfroy and the house Belmont it was bought by the Woods family and renamed Warnford Park.

The last owner was Charles Woods, who retired from the Grenadier Guards after various rowdy incidents including an explosion and went off to the Balkans as a sort of gentleman mercenary.

After the outbreak of the last war he rejoined the Army and distinguished himself, the War Office finding his specialised knowledge, topographical and military (and possibly explosive) very useful after all. The House was in Naval occupation during the Second World War and it was not until 1956 that their inevitable Nissen huts were finally demolished. The house went too. In later years the shape of the huts was oddly repeated in plastic a little way down the road as watercress began to be grown under cover in polythene tunnels.

An 18th-century coaching inn at Warnford, the Falcon, was renamed the George after George IV, who used to hunt in the neighbourhood. That sense of continuity already noted in the village has, perhaps, prompted its being renamed in recent years the George and Falcon.

# Warsash 🦢

A row of cottages built in the early 18th century on manorial "waste" shows how age brings architectural respectability. Originally four single-storey dwellings of cob sheltering in the dip—later named Claypit Bottom—which takes a stream to Hook Lake, they acquired freehold rights within 60 years or so: and in the late 18th century were faced with brick and extended. A writer who occupies one of the two homes into which the row is now divided showed me the unusually deep window-recesses resulting from the double walls. She is, I think, amused as well as pleased that the cottages have now officially reached the status of "buildings of special architectural/historic interest".

A more ambitious construction which never made the grade was a mansion built in the centre of the village in mid-Victorian times. Its water-tank was disguised in a clock-tower, which is all that remains of the building though the clock, which had ship's bells instead of chimes, was dismantled and melted down during a scrap metal drive in the Second World War. The second owner of the house, an Italian artist, played host on several occasions to King Edward VII as Prince of Wales.

That was in the days when yachting as a pastime was beginning to encroach on fishing as a livelihood. Warships had been built in Napoleonic times at Warsash—this is not the derivation of the name, incidentally: several Old English origins have been suggested, as well as ownership by the de la Warr family.

During the Second World War the boatyard became HMS *Tormentor* and was used as a training base for Commando units. The waterfront was closed off by barbed wire and a barrage balloon hovered over the river.

In the 19th century a modest fleet of fishing-boats operated out of Warsash, some constructed amidships like floating colanders with watertight bulkheads so that fish caught at sea could be kept alive in sea-water which poured through the holes as the craft sailed along. The crabs and lobsters, a speciality still commemorated in the name of a pub, were stored in artificial pools along the foreshore. For 30 years or so the pool occupants have, however, been sailing club members.

Yachting enthusiasts were among the most vociferous opponents of a plan by the American owners of the Regent Oil Company—they had been buying up farmland since 1951 until it was discovered they owned a thousand acres—to build an oil refinery opposite the Fawley petro-chemical complex originated by their rivals, Esso. After many anxious months the application was rejected in 1955 and the eastern shore of Southampton Water was declared safe for strawberry-growers, yachtsmen, and Southampton University's School of Navigation.

# West Meon

Arthur Mee wrote in 1939: "West Meon sees its river running swiftly by." Surveying the dry stream bed with a villager in the summer of 1970 I asked what had happened. He blamed the sinking of deep boreholes in the chalk higher up the valley.

There was a skirmish at West Meon during the Civil War (see Cheriton) when Royalist troops rode up with the idea of catching the Parliamentarians in church. They were too late, and the notion of preventing Waller from advancing westwards came to nothing: their move to Cheriton Wood proved disastrous.

In the churchyard is buried Thomas Lord, a Yorkshireman of Scottish descent. His headstone of 1787 describes him as "Late of Marylebone", but Lord's was the third of the cricket grounds he ran. The first, at Dorset Square, was encroached on by development and the second threatened by the construction of the Regent's Canal. Each time he was forced to move the ground he took with him the sacred turf, "the most travelled grass in London". He retired to a farm at West Meon in 1785, when he was 73. Also buried here is Guy Burgess.

In contrast, you will find modest memorials in the village hall in the form of photographs of two councillors who gave the parish nearly 90 years' service between them. Tom Edwards, a councillor for 50 years, retired in 1969 (his father Tom had been a councillor too and his son David was first elected to the council 16 years ago). Bob Russell went on the council in 1934 and when he retired owing to blindness in 1973 his wife Emma "took over" for four years.

Mr Russell was also headmaster of the village school, and many former pupils remember not only him but his cat Peter Plum, also in the photograph. It had a tendency to pad along the tops of the children's desks and rattle the inkwells, but usually ended up on the head's desk until class ended and it was time for them to walk home together.

167

# West Tisted 🪶

"A soldier, one Leiftenant Vernon, under a Gentleman, one Captayne Gibbon, of a Kentish regiment of Horse for the Parliament against the King, in the tym of ye Civil Warre between King Charles and his Parliament, being quartered at Sir Benjamin Tichborne's house, was buried in the charnell of West Tisted, on the north side, directly under the little window. He was unfortunately killed by his Captayne's Groome of his horse in the kitchen, standing by the fire. The man that did it was tried by a Councell of Warre as a thing of infortune, and not of set purpose maliciously".

Sir Benjamin was a devoted Royalist and his house was the manor, part of the Tichborne estate (in this case the name denotes both family and village). Escaping from the victorious Roundheads after the Cheriton fight (see Cheriton) he had not been home for long when Waller's troopers rode up and billeted themselves upon him. The story goes that during the whole time they were there Sir Benjamin was hiding in the priest's hole in the attic of the manor.

The parish registers from which the acount is taken are among the oldest in the country and date back to the Act which decreed registers must be kept—and to February 1538, when a John Paxton married Alis Becher.

# Weyhill 🪶

Weyhill Fair lasted, during much of the 18th century, for an entire week. Traditionally—and perhaps not surprisingly—it was the one Johnny was so long at. There was much more for a young man to do than buy his girl a bunch of blue ribbons. It was, until the last war, a sheep fair, a horse fair, a cheese fair, a hop fair, and a pleasure fair at which attractions ranged from a spotted Indian youth and a mermaid fresh from the Solent to a laughing hyena and an Algerian porcupine.

This is where Henchard got drunk and sold his wife in *The Mayor of Casterbridge*—presumably not in 1876, when a newspaper reported that "trade generally was very dull". At what was still "the largest fair in England", the number of sheep sold that October was "between 12,000 and 15,000 below the average. The so-called pleasure fair was at its zenith and, in spite of mud and filth ankle deep, the stalls were well attended".

It has been suggested that the origins of the October merry-making go much farther back than medieval times from which most fairs date. "Horning the colt" sounds a richly pagan rite but became over the centuries a ritual in which youthful new-comers to the fair had to drink strong ale from a cup fixed between two horns—perhaps originally a horn drinking vessel—while onlookers sang a very boisterous song. On the high ground west of Andover, Weyhill Fair must have been the earliest ancestor of the out-of-town hypermarket.

# Wherwell

Dead Man's Plaque (or Plack) is a local name for the 19th-century monument recalling a 10th-century murder, both in Harewood Forest on the high ground north of this valley village. Edgar the Peaceable slew—in an untypically bellicose moment—another Saxon known variously as Ethelwold or Ethelwulf. It may have been justifiable homicide since the latter having been asked by Edgar to investigate an attractive marriage prospect named Elfrida and report back, married her himself. The assassination enabled Edgar to make her his wife after all, but when he died she murdered his son by an earlier marriage so that her own son could take the throne.

Perhaps from remorse, perhaps as insurance against hellfire, she subsequently founded a nunnery in the watermeadows at Wherwell. This prospered to the point where the settlement which sprang up around it attracted wayfarers off the Roman road from Venta (Winchester) to Cunetio (Mildenhall, near Marlborough) on what might otherwise have survived as a useful direct route for 20th century traffic. Various Roman remains have been found in the neighbourhood, and in 1964 a search was mounted for the site of a watermill believed to have been among the buildings of a Romano-British homestead.

In the 13th century Elfrida's foundation flourished under the redoubtable Euphemia, a medieval Florence Nightingale of whom it is recorded that she "seemed to have the spirit of a man rather than a woman", which was presumably intended as a great compliment. Anyhow, she "with maternal piety and careful forethought built, for the use of the sick and the sound, a new and large farmery [infirmary] away from the main buildings, and in conjunction with it a dorter [dormitory] and other necessary offices. Beneath the farmery she constructed a watercourse through which a stream flowed with a sufficient force to carry off all refuse that might corrupt the air". One wonders what it did to the Test. Her rudimentary drainage system may well be responsible for the legend of the underground tunnels said to exist in what is now Priory Park.

Euphemia sounds just the person to have dealt with the Wherwell Monster, which as a blend of toad, serpent, and cockerel qualifies as a basilisk or cockatrice. It caused much consternation in the village since "all who beheld it perished" (how did anyone know what it looked like?). Eventually it committed suicide on being persuaded to look in a mirror. In another version of the story the creature, hatched by a toad from a duck's egg, lived in a cellar at the Priory, where a servant named Green claimed the reward of four acres of land for dealing with it by lowering a shining steel mirror in front of it. Waiting until it was exhausted by attacking its own reflection, he finished it off with a spear.

A WI Correspondent in *It Happened in Hampshire* adds that a four-acre piece of land in Harewood Forest is known as Green's Acres—and that "none of the older generation of inhabitants could be induced to eat a duck's egg".

Both versions have an odd echo of the Classical legend of the slaying of the Gorgon which literally petrified its attackers, turning them to stone as they looked at it. Perseus slew it by using a metal shield as a mirror, so that all he saw was his own reflection fighting that of the monster.

Within a century of Euphemia's hygienic reign at the Priory, however, the goings-on there were so scandalous that the Bishop—William of Wykeham—decreed that neither cleric nor layman should avail himself of a night's lodging with the sisters.

Presumably it was for military rather than for moral reasons that the Puritans took some potshots at the building which in their time stood on the Priory site. The White Lion used to have two cannon balls by way of mementoes, but one disappeared during the Second World War: suspicion fell on some souvenir-hunting GI.

Two tree stories. When a fir in the Priory grounds blew down in a gale, the roots were found to enclose the skeleton of a man. A treasure supposed to be buried near by was never found—just as well, since the discoverer could, according to legend, expect only sudden death. Perhaps it was guarded by a basilisk.

By 1956 the Pound Tree, a 300-year-old elm which had sheltered animals in the village pound, was a hollow shell six feet in diameter at the base. According to one of the workmen called in to fell it as dangerous, it even rocked when pushed. As it fell a limb weighing half a ton or so split away from the main trunk and demolished the war memorial. This recorded the names of all those from the village who had fought; whether they had died or returned safely. Within the hour Mr William Harding, whose name was one of those inscribed on it, died at his home a few yards away in the High Street.

171

Its row of timber-framed thatched cottages makes Wherwell one of Hampshire's most-photographed villages. Few of those who make appreciatative noises at their appearance realise that a forgotten railway runs along the wooded ridge above and behind them (see Longparish). When it closed 20 years ago Wherwell Station was converted into an unusual form of housing by Andover Rural Council (in 1963 I interviewed a family happily occupying what had been the booking office and station loos), and private houses were built—one by the council clerk—on the level stretch where the track had widened out into a goods yard overlooking the Test.

# Whitchurch

The historical development of many towns and villages is dictated by their road and river patterns, and this is particularly true of Whitchurch. A corn mill is listed in the Domesday Book, an on its site was built in about 1800 one of several woollen mills. The local speciality was shalloons, a kind of worsted named after Chalons in France. Within 100 years the mill was producing silk and not wool, with power coming since 1930 from electricity not the water-wheel. Today when a barrister "takes silk" his gown may well be made of silk hand-stitched in Whitchurch—the home, incidentally, of the Master of the Rolls, Lord Denning.

Bere Mill, known as Bare Mill when it was "built by Jane, the widow of Tho. Deane, Esquire, in the year 1710", was where Henri de Portal started producing banknotes in 1719 before transferring to new premises (see Laverstoke and Overton) six years later. As Huguenot refugees the Portals were Protestants and the tradition of religious dissent seems to have been strong in Whitchurch. A "Protestant Dissenters' Chapel" erected in 1705 was followed by buildings for Methodists of several different persuasions; for "Peculiar Baptists"; and for "Followers of Joe Smith, commonly called Mormonists". At the end of the century there were frequent clashes between rival brands of Christians, with attacks on Salvation Army meetings. Sectarian violence resulted in people being taken to court for breach of the peace, and somebody even wrote to

Queen Victoria complaining about the establishment of a popish hierarchy. However, peace broke out eventually: one chapel was even turned into a jam-factory. Its tall chimney was taken down, brick by brick, in 1964.

There was also some dissension within the Established Church. Curfew was observed right up to the 19th century, and the bell-ringer lived in a tied cottage which belonged to the church. He could not be turned out so long as he performed his regular duties, but 150 years ago the ecclesiastical authorities wanted to sell the cottage with vac. pos. So muttering something to the effect that Curfew Shall Not Ring Tonight, the vicar barred and bolted the church door thus ensuring that, since the ringer couldn't get into the church, he could be got out of his cottage.

It would be nice to think that it might have been required for a couple of whom it was recorded about that time: "Monday was married at Whitchurch Mr Moses Edney of Charlecot to Miss Jane Hayter of Whitchurch after a courtship of 24 years."

In Elizabethan times (and later) the correct name for Hampshire was The County of Southampton. This explains, if it does not justify, the plodding metre of an epitaph in the church which begins:

This grave (Oh grief) hath swallowed up with wide and
open mouth
The body of good Richard Brooke of Whitchurch,
Hampton South.

Its position at the crossing of busy routes, between London and the West, and between the Midlands and the South Coast, meant that Whitchurch was an interchange point on stage-coach routes. Passengers from Oxford bound, for instance, for the West country would stay at the White Hart while awaiting the Exeter stage from London. Railway travellers later probably had to do the same, since plans to connect the north–south line (see East Woodhay) with the east–west route never materialised. Nowadays north–south road traffic avoids the steep descent on the old road from Newbury by taking the bypass—one of several influences which over the years have counteracted the trend to urbanisation.

Until 1832 Whitchurch did return two Members to Parliament but it was never—although it had a titular mayor—incorporated as a borough. The Court Leet was abandoned with the mayoralty in 1866 of Mr Spencer Clarke but was revived for the Festival of Britain in 1951 when his grandson, Mr John Spencer Clarke, acted as mayor during the celebrations.

# Whitsbury ❧

High up against the Wiltshire border, Whitsbury has seen human settlement since pre-Roman days. The "castle" and its ditches on the chalk downland are the remains of a Romano-British system of defences against Saxons invading from the south. Now the downs provide gallops for racehorses: earlier, the speciality was pigs, with an annual Hog Fair which lasted until 1825.

# Wickham ❧

Birthplace in 1324 of Bishop William of—in the spelling of the day—Wykeham, it had by then been holding its famous annual fair for over half a century. Exactly when the tradition began of starting the proceedings by giving a pony a pint of beer is difficult to pinpoint, but it was in 1949 that the bonfire celebrations were transferred from the Square to the Recreation Ground. This was because the heat of the 1948 fire was so great that shop windows were cracked and the insurance companies declined to pay up.

The oldest building in the largely Georgian Square, for many years a curio shop, dates back to the 16th century. The bank which acquired it applied in 1968 for permission to demolish it, despite the fact that one room contained some rare and beautiful painted plasterwork believed to be the oldest in Hampshire. Reopened as a wine-bar by someone with a greater sense of art and history, it has been restored to something nearer its original condition.

Wickham was described several centuries ago as "a praty

townlet" but its expansion was, paradoxically, made difficult by the coming of the railway. The Meon Valley Line, more effectively than the river itself, came between the village and its church, and expansion eastwards just didn't happen. Possibly another reason was the existence of the Rookesbury estate, which with over 1,000 acres of coverts was reckoned in Edwardian times to be one of the greatest sporting estates in the South of England. Formerly the residence of the Garniers (the family spanned the distance from Huguenot immigrant to Lord Lieutenant of Hampshire) the house is now a school.

At one time the course of the Meon used to be regularly diverted so as to produce a harvest of stranded fish. This must presumably have been below Chesapeake Mill, rebuilt and renamed by John Prior, miller, with timber he bought in 1820 from the American man-o'-war *Chesapeake*—bested seven years earlier, as the ballad relates, by HMS *Shannon* in the War of Independence.,

Another bankside industry, a tanyard, eventually provided a site for an early experiment in street lighting by acetylene. The original lamps were not finally disposed of until 1950: but that was too early, I suppose, for anyone but a scrap-metal merchant to have taken an interest in what nowadays we know as industrial archaeology.

By 1971 the tide had turned and the Meon Valley Locomotive Society planned to transform Wickham Station into a Museum of Steam. It had been unused for 16 years. Within 16 weeks of being approached, British Rail bulldozed the buildings without even telling the Society.

# Woodgreen 🌿

One of several settlements on the fringes of the New Forest—alluvial pockets round small streams provide better soil than the uncultivatable open heath—Woodgreen is distinguished from the others by its village hall. This is for artistic and sociological reasons rather than architectural. When the building was erected 50 years ago two artists, R. W. Baker and E. R. Payne, enlivened the interior walls with murals depicting village people, and their animals, at work and play.

The apple harvest is one theme: in earlier days it might have been cherry-picking on Merry Days (merries—see Chandler's Ford—were a kind of cherry, from the French *merise*). The trouble was that crowds of people turned up to pick and eat the cherries—and to take a drink or two as well. Riotous behaviour is said to have prompted a teetotaller to buy up the merry gardens and put an end to the festivities.

Part of the trouble may have been that the village had a reputation for lawlessness anyhow—being on the forest edge it had attracted squatters, some of whom were avoiding not only minor regulations but authority in general. At one time, fighting between Woodgreeners and lads from neighbouring parishes led to the place being nicknamed "Ireland".

This may surprise those familiar with the prim cottages and neat gardens which today line the little network of lanes between the forest and the Avon. Both used to provide materials and incentives for one cottage industry—the making of eel traps from split hazel.

# The Worthies ❧

Upstream from Winchester, the Worthies lie along the course of the Itchen—Headbourne Worthy, King's Worthy, Abbot's Worthy, and Martyr Worthy. The parish church at Headbourne is, like the cathedral at Winchester, dedicated to St Swithun—and another link between village and city is the brass memorial to John Kent, a chorister who went to the college there in 1431 and died, still a schoolboy, in 1434. Much of the church is even older and predates the Norman conquest. When it was enlarged in the 15th century a rood-screen was carved on what had been an outside wall, but the figures on it were mutilated when Bishop Horne (1560–80) ordered that crucifixes in churches all over the diocese of Winchester should be destroyed as idolatrous.

The Worthies lost something of their village atmosphere with the building of the Great Western railway line connecting the Midlands and the south by way of Newbury and Winchester (see East Woodhay and Whitchurch), then the Winchester bypass, and finally the Newbury link road which runs partly along the old GWR route. Thanks largely to the Itchen they manage to retain something of the past in spite of the inevitable changes caused by their proximity to expanding Winchester.

Harking back can, however, be a source of profit rather than an empty form of nostalgia. Ten years or so ago two old cast-iron firebacks were found buried on the site of a foundry at Kings Worthy. They were used to produce boot-scrapers, tongs, pokers, and other items for "fireplace sets" to be sold in this country and abroad. When the local evening paper printed a photograph in 1976 of men at work in the rebuilt foundry a man wrote from Eastbourne recalling his boyhood memories of what were then—in the first decade of this century—the Vulcan Ironworks. He confessed: "We used to wait until the works closed, then, with my older brothers and other boys, I would go to the works and from the mountains of old iron there, we would rake out the old bicycles and have great fun trying to ride them. There were old penny-farthings, bone-shakers with solid tyres, and other ancient bikes that today would be worth a lot of money."

At least their original riders didn't get into the same trouble as the early motorists who, until the speed limit was raised to 20 mph in 1904, were frequently fined for "scorching" between King's Worthy and Basingstoke. It was in 1903 that a defendant accused of travelling at 23 mph said he'd rather not give his name as he had a distinguished passenger aboard. The chairman of the magistrates, told by a police witness that the gentleman in question was Arthur Balfour, fined the driver £5 and said of his passenger: "Now perhaps the Prime Minister will change the law." No doubt the Act of the following year was just a coincidence. . . .

# Yateley 🦡

One of Guy Fawkes' fellow-conspirators in the Gunpowder Plot of 1605 was Francis Tresham, whose sister was married to Lord Mounteagle of Yateley. A letter believed to have been sent by Tresham, but in the handwriting of his servant William Vavasour, advised His Lordship on October 26th "to devyse some excuse to shift of his attendance at this Parliament, for God and man hathe concurred to punish the wickedness of this tyme. He should retyre into the country and there expect the event. There shall receive a terrible blowe this Parliament, and yet they shall not see who hurts them. The danger will be passed as soon as he has burned this letter".

The name Monteagle Farm today recalls the man whose decision to show King James' ministers the anonymous warning resulted in the arrest of the conspirators and the saving of His Majesty's life. It brought His Lordship no thanks: in fact some people suspected him of complicity in the plot and of fabricating the letter to save his skin.

A main-road village between London and the south–west, Yateley had its share of highwaymen. One of the most notorious—his name is commemorated in Derby Green—was a part-timer, Parson Derby. His Reverence disobeyed not only the eighth commandment by robbing wayfarers, but the sixth by shooting the driver of a mailcoach when he refused to stop, and possibly also the seventh, since he is said to have been betrayed by one of a number of ladies he fancied. He was eventually hanged for armed robbery and murder not far from the inn—now Yew Tree Cottage—where he used to await the arrival of the London stage.

Another rogue who lived in the parish, probably at Minley Warren, was Colonel Thomas Blood. Having in 1670 or 1671 failed to assassinate the Lord Lieutenant of Ireland, whom he blamed for the loss of his Irish estate, he managed some months later to knock down the keeper of the Crown Jewels and make off with them, but dropped the lot when his horse stumbled. Somehow he talked his way into not only a royal pardon—he could have expected the death penalty for treason—but into the restoration of his property in Ireland, which brought him in £300 a year.

Two hundred years later a third robber, Charlie Peace, rented a cottage in Moulsham Lane under the name of David Ward, but fled when workmen he had engaged came across some of his loot in the trunk of a tree in the garden.

Up against the Surrey border, Yateley is in the military area which straddles the county boundary. Minley Manor, taken over by the Army in 1936, had been rebuilt in 1860 as a

Victorian variation on the French château theme. The result is a conglomeration of turrets and pinnacles, startling even by the standards of that dottily exuberant period of architecture.

Contrastingly functional buildings house Yateley Industries, which were started as workshops for disabled girls in 1937 but closed for the duration of the Second World War. From their purpose-built post-war premises are produced block-printed textiles of bold and pleasing designs which I remember vividly from a visit with a television crew in the 'sixties.

Maying and mumming (see Boldre) were two traditions kept up in Yateley until the 20th century. The May Day garlands which the village girls made featured a doll carried from house to house in a wicker framework. By the time this ancient pagan rite had become Christianised the little figure stood for the Virgin Mary.

The mummers' play was a fairly elaborate version containing not only one turkey snipe, or Turkish Knight, but two. As this is the last entry in our Hampshire alphabet, I'll end with a quotation:

SECOND TURKEY SNIPE:
Is this all true, Doctor, what thou has been talking about?

DOCTOR:
Yes, I am not one of those little quack doctors to go about telling you this thing and that thing, who would tell you as many lies in five minutes as I would in seven years!

## BACKGROUND READING

Much of the material in this book is drawn from the files of the *Southern Evening Echo* and I am grateful to both Southern Newspapers PLC for permission to make use of its library and to the librarian, Peter Ashton, and his colleagues for their patience and help. Tony Richards, district librarian at Southampton, and his staff at the Civic Centre, were equally forbearing and forthcoming.

The fact that *It Happened in Hampshire*, compiled by members of Women's Institutes all over the county, has been re-printed five times since its original publication in 1936 confirms my belief that anyone interested in Hampshire's past should find room for a copy on his shelves. If it is true that history is what our grandparents remember this is Hampshire's most delightful history book!

Many villages have been fortunate in having residents sufficiently interested and industrious to ferret through records and talk to old inhabitants in order to write books about their particular parish. I have acknowledged these publications at appropriate points in the text but should like to make particular mention of *Meonstoke and Soberton* by F. B. Collins and J. C. Hurst (Winton Publications, Winchester) which is a model of its kind.

Of books about the county in general I particularly enjoyed, during my refresher-reading, *Hampshire*—in the series published by Batsford. The author, Ralph Dutton, is a former High Sheriff whose knowledge of, and devotion to, the county in which he lives emerges in so much of his writing—including *Hinton Ampner: a Hampshire Manor*, a history of his own home.

In 1979 Hampshire County Planning Department published *Hampshire's Heritage—and a Policy for its Future*. Do not be tempted to write this off as a stilted discussion document: it is a most imaginatively presented compilation which conveys the flavour of the county's past in pictures and paragraphs before summarising the problems which our much-maligned planners have to face.

Since the first edition of this book appeared the Council's Recreation Department has published John H. Holder's admirably practical and comprehensive *Explore Hampshire*—coast and countryside, museums and parks, industrial archaeology and nature trails.

Phillimore of Chichester have published two books which deserve the attention of anyone interested in the county's past: *A History of Hampshire*, by Barbara Carpenter Turner, and *Hampshire Harvest—a Traveller's Notebook* by Robert F. W. Potter. R. L. P. and Dorothy Jowett's book *The Solent and its Surroundings* is published by Terence Dalton of Lavenham.

Earlier books may be hard to find, and their contents unsubstantiated by later research, but some have been reprinted recently in facsimile editions as deserving discriminating interest. Among them is T. W. Shore's 1892 *History of Hampshire* (republished in 1976 by EP of Wakefield). I am lucky to possess the original 1909 edition of Telford Varley's *Hampshire*, with illustrations by Wilfrid Ball, given to me by a former colleague, the late Freddy Judd. His name also adorns the flyleaf of my *Highways and Byways in Hampshire*, D. H. Moutray Read's guide of 1908.

L. Collison Morley's *Companion into Hampshire* (Spurbooks, 1973), Martin Thornhill's *Explorer's Hampshire* (Skeffington, 1952) and Alan Rannie's *The Winchester Countryside* (Allen & Unwin, 1947) all helped to fill in the background of a most rewarding landscape.

Finally, it would be churlish not to acknowledge the pleasure I have derived from looking through numerous published collections of old photographs including John Norwood's *Victorian and Edwardian Hampshire* (Batsford, 1973) and *Hambledon and Denmead* by Terry Norman (Bay Tree Publishing, Alresford, 1976).

# Index